CONTENTS

Printed by:
Gunnarshaug A/S

Graphic design:
Arnfinn Faltinsen
and Lars Chr. Sande

Typesetting:
Gunnarshaug

Paper: 150 g Imperial
from Papierfabrik Scheufelen

ISBN 82991014-25

Inside cover, front:
The Suldal steamer
Photograph: Inge Bruland

Inside cover, back:
Salmon fishing at Suldalslågen
Photograph: Inge Bruland

Above:
Egerøy lighthouse
Photograph: Johan Aakre

Next page:
Yrkjesfjorden
Photograph: Leif Berge

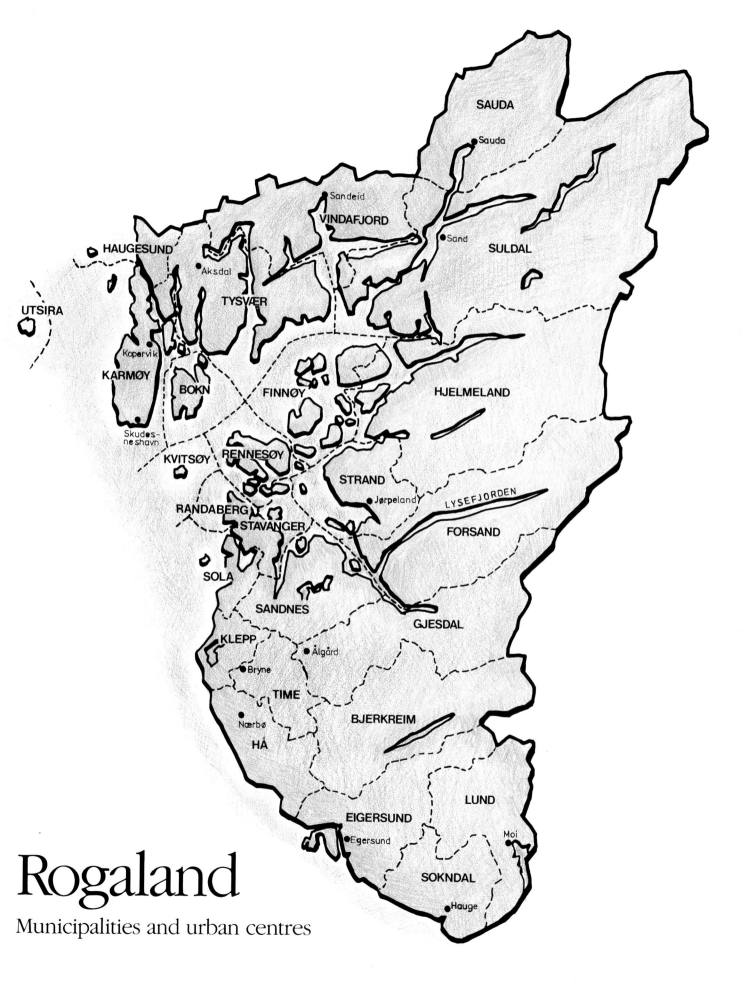

SAUDA
• Sauda

• Sandeid

VINDAFJORD
• Sand

SULDAL

HAUGESUND

• Aksdal

TYSVÆR

UTSIRA

• Kopervik

KARMØY

BOKN

FINNØY

HJELMELAND

Skudes-
neshavn

KVITSØY

RENNESØY

STRAND

• Jørpeland

LYSEFJORDEN

RANDABERG

STAVANGER

FORSAND

SOLA

SANDNES

GJESDAL

KLEPP

• Ålgård

• Bryne

TIME

BJERKREIM

• Nærbø

HÅ

LUND

EIGERSUND

• Moi

• Egersund

SOKNDAL

• Hauge

Rogaland

Municipalities and urban centres

ROGALAND
A many faceted county

Editor
Lars Chr. Sande

English edition
Susan Tyrrell

Greetings from the chairman
of the county council of Rogaland

*You are holding in your hands a book with
over 300 full colour photographs. Never
before has there been anything to compare
to this work on Rogaland – a county that
has made greater strides in development
than any other in Norway. But in the midst
of all the progress Rogaland has kept much
of its special charm; the old and the new
live side by side harmoniously in this many
faceted county. We believe that a fondness
for Rogaland can only be enhanced by this
book.*

Rogaland County Council
Gunnarshaug

Smoke signals from the Vista Cave

The best known stone age cave in Norway is *Vistehåla* in the municipality of Randaberg. This is where our ancestors lived some 6000 years ago, in 50 sq.m. plus kitchen. The ascending smoke in the photograph is a symbol of all that has been cooked in this cave through the centuries.

As for the cave dwellers, most of their waking hours must have been given to gathering food. Digging into the compost heaps of their past we see that their diet included birds and fish.

Archaeological excavations prove that the Vistehåla cave was inhabited from the time of the mass migrations, around the year 500.

Photograph: Kyllingstad/Furenes.

History
Pages 54–73

Local self-government for 150 years

The signals emanating from Rogaland when the county celebrated the 150th anniversary of local government were considerably stronger than the smoke signals on the preceding page. The Stavanger Brassband and the Lunde-haugen school choir played a rhapsody written by Petr Cejka, and folk songs from the area. 130 young singers and musicians filled the stage at the Stavanger Concert Hall. There was much to celebrate in the progress of the 26 municipalities and the county council since the law of local self-government was passed on January 14, 1837.

Municipalities
Pages 193–216

From a modest beginning, great strides in development.
Photograph: Jan B. Henriksen.

A foundation of herring bones

It is said that Haugesund is built upon herring bones. Without the rich herring catch and the salting sheds on every point of land, there may never have been a town by the Smedasund. Other Rogaland towns were dependent on herring as well. When they failed, the economy toppled and many merchants went bankrupt.

Gradually, when it looked darkest for the fishing fleet, Rogaland found other foundations for her economy.

Herring is still salted in Haugesund, but now it is herring as a delicacy, rather than herring as day-to-day monotony.

Photograph: Terje Størkesen.

Economy
Pages 96–125

Rogaland sets the table

In the old days in Rogaland there used to be fried herring and boiled herring, salt herring and dried herring, herring cakes and pickled herring and then some more herring for dinner. It was called "silver from the sea" and was aheaped up in shining mountains, to serve as the very foundation of life.

Rogaland has come a long way, to be able to set a table like this. Right at home we find the basis for a richly varied diet, and even for gourmet adventures. In addition to having become a supplier of food, Rogaland also manufactures high quality kitchen utensils and crockery, adding a touch of style to modern housekeeping.

Photograph: Jonas Friestad.

The food of Rogaland
Pages 177–192

11

The work-a-day oil industry

When the first huge oil constructions such as the Ekofisk tank were towed out to sea, the entire town followed the process intently. But, as the years pass, mammoth constructions have become a part of daily life and so numerous that most people no longer keep track.

You don't hear much talk about the "oil adventure" any more. For most Rogalanders high level activity has become matter of fact. We tend to take it all for granted, it takes visitors from beyond Rogaland to really notice.

Not that there weren't landmarks of magnitude even before the discovery of oil. The silos in the background belong to Felleskjøpet Agder Rogaland – the Agder Rogaland co-operative of farmers – with a turnover of 1,4 billion kroner in 1986. Within Norwegian agriculture this is the largest turnover for a year – showing the importance of Rogaland farming on national scale.

The oil-county
Pages 126–149

Landing in Rogaland

There is good reason to land in Rogaland. Stavanger Airport is one of the most modern in Europe, mainly thanks to the new terminal building, inaugurated on the airport's 50th anniversary in May, 1987.

Stavanger Airport was the first civilian airport in Norway.

Boat traffic has been important to Rogaland's fjord-divided county. Our access to the east has been a railway connection since 1944. The major cross country highways are mostly of good standard.

Photograph: Egil Eriksson.

Communication
Pages 150–161

Beach art – Sola 1986

The dream of arranging an art exhibition on Sola beach came true for a couple of artists, Pia Myrvold and Randy Naylor, in the summer of 1986. It was a time to let the imagination free. An "experience platform" was erected and the most remarkable constructions appeared along the beach and the dunes, old, painted such as rowboats standing on end.

The event provoked controversy; some were delighted, others annoyed. The exhibition will not be soon forgotten.

Photograph: Per Jonsson.

Culture
Pages 74–95

Be our guest

The recent years have seen an explosion in hotel and restaurant building in Rogaland. The Hotel Maritim in Haugesund, for example, stands ready to welcome either individuals, or whole congresses. The hotel has become known as the home of the Film Festival and the Amanda awards.

Photograph: Tor Brekke.

Tourism
Pages 162–176

From around the world

People from 80 different nations now live in Rogaland, so it is fair to say they come to our coast from the world over. Ten percent of the population of Stavanger are immigrants, adding to the cultural diversity.

Ethiopian Dibetu Galeta, with the market in the background, comes to Stavanger from East Africa, the cradle of humanity. Considering we all stem from her ancestors, it is not a long step towards accepting our global brotherhood.

Photograph: Jonas Friestad.

Immigrants
Pages 244–253

Great moments

VIP's tend to visit Stavanger fairly often because of the oil industry. One of these great moments was the visit of Queen Elizabeth II. Along with her came H.M. King Olav and Prince Phillip.

Arne Rettedal was mayor of Stavanger at the time.

The weather co-operated. Summer arrived along with the Queen. When the royal yacht Britannia left Stavanger harbour, it was King Olav photographing the photographers.

Photograph: Egil Eriksson.

Highlights
Pages 218–243

The sea

"Nothing is as roomy as the sea, nothing as patient. Like a good-natured elephant it carries upon its broad back the petty concerns of this world; there is room within its vast and cool depths for all our wails. It is not so that the sea is faithless, for it has never promised anything: without demands, without obligations, free, pure and genuine beats its great heart – the last sound one in a tainted world." From Alexander Kielland's "Garmand & Worse", 1880.

Over a hundred years later we can no longer take Kiellands words for granted. It is we who have an obligation: to keep that sea untainted.

Photo: Allan Sande.

Nature
Pages 34–53

Bird's eye view of four Rogaland towns

Four towns in Rogaland owe their expansion to the particular circumstances of their regions. Southernmost is **Egersund,** pages 26 and 27, which prospered because of its sheltered harbour and rich fishing. Egersund's hey day as a seafaring town was in the era of the tall ships. Even without *Fayancefabrikk* – the pottery factory – the town continues to do well.

Photograph: Norsk Fly og Flyfoto A/S.

Sandnes stood, literally, on feet of clay, pages 28 and 29. But they were strong enough to bear her weight and support an industry based upon it. Other industry followed, making Sandnes an important industrial and commercial centre.

Photograph: Norsk Fly og Flyfoto A/S.

Stavanger is so spread out that an aerial photograph needs to be taken from a great height in order to get the whole town in. This photograph, pages 30 and 31, taken by Statoil's photographer Leif Berge in the early hours of the morning is already a classic. it allows individual fantasy free play.

Haugesund, pages 32 and 33, grew thanks to the schools of herring that visited this coast year after year. The settlement first hugged the Smedasund, then extended in growing circles as new development added to the old in this well groomed town.

Foto: Leif Berge

Rogaland Nature

By: Per Frøyland Pallesen

The residents below Helleren in Jøssingfjord managed to do without roof tiles.

Following page, top: Jøssingfjord.

Below: Dalane coast, looking northwest. In the distance, the Fokkstein islands outside Jøssingfjord.

Photograph: Rune Roaldkvam

The nature of Rogaland is the fount of enormous variety and changes of mood, even within short distances. In a fairly limited area we have a coast that is alive with sea birds, sandy beaches, fertile plains and rich wetlands, undulating hills, forests, a mild and sheltered archipelago, mighty valleys and dramatic fjords – plus heights that reach into eternal snow and ice. Harsh and weatherbeaten on the coast, wild and lovely inland, but laced with sheltered nooks safe from even the worst of west coast weather.

Four totally different geographic regions dominate, with different types of bedrock, sedimentation, landscape, flora and fauna. These vastly different facets of nature have given an identity of their own to each of the four regions and to their inhabitants.

From Åna-Sira to Ørsdal

Dalane is characterised by its bedrock: a starved feldspar called anorthosite. This almost white mineral has been eroded by ice and water into a lumpy landscape with steep,

At Nordre Sund in Eigersund a stretch of mellowness is reminiscent of the Southland. *Per Frøyland Pallesen*

finely polished heights, but with relatively shallow depths. Small valleys lying in disarray are marked by a confusion of lakes and rivers; unusual for Norway.

It is a fascinating landscape. Reactions can range from delight to mistrust, but it leaves few indifferent.

A belt of more fertile norite spreads from the coast at Rekefjord to Sokndal, introducing a marked contrast: lush vegetation fills the relatively narrow and sheltered valleys. This is where Southland and Westland meet, in a jumble of growth. Some of the forests are reserves, full of oak, lime, elm and black elder, as well as pine and spruce scattered through the deciduous forests.

Rekefjord's norite has its uses in technology. Much of it is exported. Anorthosite also has a multitude of uses, its white colour is used from toothpaste to detergents. The size and number of quarries at Hellvik indicate the demand. There are other riches too: the Tellnes mines at Hauge are the largest source of titanium in Europe.

The Dalane coast is out of the ordinary as well, the abrupt and naked bedrock cliffs have their closest parallels at Stadt and the North Cape. They can be an anxiety-filled challenge for pleasure craft making their way to the South Coast but even here, on the inland side of Eigerøy, are sheltered, wooded bays with public recreation areas.

This is the spot where the Bjerkreim watershed's mighty valleys run out. The inland ice has accumulated much sedimentation here. Huge moraine masses have been modelled by the ice flow, shaping one unusual formation after the other; text book examples of how melting ice forms landscape. Most remarkable is perhaps the snake shaped gravel ridge of St. Olavsormen, a relic of the time when the water system ran underground to Hellvik. It has been named a "site of special scientific interest".

East of the Bjerkreim river is characteristic West coast landscape with a number of straight, parallel valleys with steep sides and deep fjords. Of the lakes, the one at Ørsdal is the biggest. The terrain climbs towards the east to about 1000 metres, rich in topsoil and vegetation. This is sheep country, the major one in Norway.

The hills of Bjerkreim abound in moors, birch forests and sheltered waters alternating with wild gullies and rapids. Birds of prey live here. This area is becoming the main winter abode of the Scandinavian golden eagle. Lower down in the ice-free waters, flocks of whooper swans spend the winter now and then.

Above: The farm complex at Tengs in Eigersund has much history behind it. Many of the old houses have been restored. Tengs is surrounded by the sort of nature to evoke Beethoven's "Pastorale", Symphony.

Fotlandsfossen (to the right) is the main challenge for salmon along the Bjerkreim watershed, eased eventually by the "salmon steps".

Kvitladalen in Bjerkreim.

Photograph: Per Frøyland Pallesen.

The landscape of Jæren has inspired artists from home and abroad. The painting on this page, named "Fra Ogne", was done by Kitty Kielland, sister of the famous Stavanger writer.

From Revtangen to the Frafjord hills

The Jæren landscape is as obviously rich as the Dalane landscape is improverished. This flat, fertile moraine along Norway's southwestern corner is atypical in every way; for Rogaland, and for the rest of the country.

The coastline is unusual enough, with an interplay of shiningly polished round boulders at the base of a well formed moraine profile, and restless sand dunes covered in malmgrass. Jæren has the country's finest sandy beaches, all of them nature reserves except for a section on the coast of Sola and Stavanger.

Gently sloping naked rock shelters little bays around the southern and the northern Jæren beaches. Migratory birds choose these and the inland lakes in this area for a respite on their journey between the Arctic and southern Europe. Most of them continue on their way, but some remain and spend the winter. A section of rough, rocky – and inaccessible for man – coastline here gives shelter to Norway's kittiwake, fulmar and cormorant.

Rogaland is Norway's foremost bird county with around 360 species registered in 1987. Some 270 different birds have been sighted in the Orre-Reve area alone.

Plant life is out of the ordinary as well. Rare species still abound wherever the plough and fertilizer have not reached. Little of Jæren's original landscape of heather, wetlands and moors has been conserved, only a few small segments are protected. Except for a few picturesque spots on the heights of High Jæren, even the peat bogs have almost disappeared.

The climate and the quality of the soil here help push agricultural yield towards the highest in the world. Livestock density is the highest in the world, however this is not sheer blessing: water resources are strained and major environmental problems abound as a consequence. Every effort is being made to cleanse the rivers, to justify the claim that these are among the country's best for salmon fishing.

Between Low Jæren and the inland hills rises a wall of granite, extending east of Gandsfjord and towards the south.

The open valleys and steep mountains west of Høgsfjord abound in lakes and forests, berries and mushrooms, small game and much fish: trout, char, gwyniad and eel.

East of Høgsfjord-Dirdal is again a typical Westland scene. The Hunnedal and Frafjordal valleys cut through the tall massive of bedrock with practically vertical cliff sides, waterfalls and rapids. The road through the ski slopes of Giljastølen towards Frafjord is an example of Norwegian nature at its dramatic best. The highlight in this area the 90 metre free fall of the Månafossen water fall, biggest in this part of Norway. The falls form a gateway to the Frafjord mountains, full of variety and practically undisturbed by man, only one and a half hour by car from Stavanger.

To the north, Hunnedal is Rogaland's most pupular winter sport area, with stable snow conditions.

On the following page, top, a resplendent day at Orre beach in Klepp. The Jæren beaches are nature reserves.
Below: a beach of round boulders serving as foreground to Feinstein Fyr lighthouse.   Photograph: Odd Inge Worsøe

Orrevatnet is one of Norway's most important wetlands.   *Photograph: Rune Roaldkvam*

About two thirds of Rogaland's population live on Jæren. At the same time, this stretch of fertile flatlands is one of Norway's most important agricultural areas. This means that Jæren's urban centres are surrounded by farms and that there is a scarcity of recreational areas. Along the coast and in the foothills are several fine spots for enjoying nature, and these are used by a large number of people, year around.

Overall, outdoor recreation and farming live side by on Jæren. So, it is important for people to be well informed about which places are suitable for recreation and the rules which apply to the use of the outdoors. This has been one of the objectives of the Jæren outdoor recreation council in establishing the "Open Air House" at Orre: to inform about nature preservation in the district and to influence people's attitudes about their use of nature.

Opposite: Månefossen in Gjesdal.   Per Frøyland Pallesen
Next page: Fossgjuvet in Røssdalen, Forsand.
                          Photograph: Kjell Helle Olsen
"Friluftshuset" – the Open Air House. The Orresand information centre for conservation and recreation.
                          Photograph: Per Frøyland Pallesen

Looking south from Ystebøhavn on Kvitsøy.   Photograph: Rune Roaldkvam

From Kvitsøy to Vassdalseggen

The Ryfylke region represents a typical cross-section of West Coast landscape.

Furthest west lie the weathered islands of Kvitsøy, one for each day of the year, it is said. They are naked and treeless but have a shist nutrient that supports a rich flora wherever the sheep do not reach. The original sedimentary deposits of clay and limestone have been much altered by closeness to the formation of the caledonian mountain chain.

The outer islands and skerries are full of sea birds and seals are also to be seen – rather too frequently in the view of fishermen.

Further inland in the Boknafjord basin are the vast, fertile "slate islands" which are responsible for the succesful agriculture of the Ryfylke islands.

Some of the rock is vulcanic of origin, resistant to erosion. Because of this it often appears hat-like, as a steep crown of smooth rock, surrounded by a brim of loose stone and moraine.

There is soapstone here as well, which has gone into the construction of Utstein Kloster, the Cathedral in Stavanger and other medieval buildings. Marble and slate has also been quarried here.

There is much to remind one of Scotland and further north, in the Ryfylke islands. The use of stone for building, and especially the stone walls between the fields, point to a common cultural background. The area around Utstein Kloster is a particularly lovely one.

Climate improves rapidly as you move deeper into the Boknafjord basin. The vegetation reflects the warmer summers, milder winters and higher lime content of the soil in this region – the best of which are the Stjernerøy islands. The most profuse vegetation appears to be ivy, holly and honeysuckle but there is also a large variety of colourful and sometimes rare flowers. The flora of this region is as plentiful as in the lime-rich areas of the Oslo fjord. Some of the richest growth is found on North Talgje, part of which is a nature reserve.

The Boknafjord basin is a boat-owner's holiday paradise. It is full of tiny islets, bays and sounds which are sheltered and offer delightfull harbours for ever-growing numbers of pleasure boats.

A number of parallel fjords cut sharply into the mass of bedrock from Boknafjord towards the north east. Ice from inland has flowed towards the sea fairly effortlessly along the fissures in the mountains. The cliffs plunge steeply into

Utstein Abbey on Rennesøy.   Photograph: Per Frøyland Pallesen

*To the left: Rennesøy, looking towards Mosterøy and North Jæren.
Photograph: Rune Roaldkvam*

*Centre: A heaven for pleasure craft in the Ryfylke, here at the North
Talgje nature reserve and recreation area.
Photograph: Per Frøyland Pallesen*

*From Hylen in Hylsfjorden, Suldal.
Photograph: Per Frøyland Pallesen*

the fjords and the ice has carved "over-deepenings" or canyons in the fjords.

Lysefjord is the undisputed queen of these fjords. It is a 40 kilometre long "corridor of rock" as Victor Hugo called it, with faceted vertical cliff sides of polished granite. *Preke-stolen* – the Pulpit Rock – has become a trademark for Rogaland tourism, but the fjord has far more to offer. The most imposing is possibly *Kjeragveggen* –the Kjeragwall –a kilometre high vertical rock wall which plunges into the fjord. It is only a few years ago that Kjeragveggen was first scaled by mountain climbers.

Beyond the fjords are flat and fertile valleys. The plentiful watershed has now mostly been channelled underground and harnessed for power. However, a few salmon rivers still remain: the Espedal river runs free, as do the Vormo and Hålandsåna. In the Årdal area every effort is made to keep the remaining watershed, and to revive the landscape and the river for sport fishing.

The county's most beautiful valley, without doubt, is Suldal and Suldalslågen, where enough of the original water system remains undisturbed for the landscape to have retained its natural aspect. Rich, well kept farms line the valley. The salmon fishing is legendary here; enthusiastically and elegantly practiced for some 150 years.

Above Suldalsvatnet however, power development has left its mark. Not only are large portions of the mountain dammed but the hydrography of the region has actually

The balcony of The Pulpit Rock, surveying the Lysefjord below.   *Photograph: Odd Inge Worøe*

been reversed to serve three of the country's largest power stations, located in this region. The plateau of the Ryfylke reaches 1000-1200 metres, and drops almost vertically to the fjords. A hydroelectric engineer's dream come true. Unarguably, the energy created is of great value, but much has been lost along the way.

Important parts of the area are still fortunately untouched, and may be eventually protected. So far, only the Vormo watershed, a relatively small one and a minor contribution to the county's energy supply, has been named a reserve. It is a mixture of the typical and the rare in both geology and the plant life on it. To the east, Lusaheia's polished bedrock plateau stands in contrast to the rolling hills.

North of the huge Blåsjø reservoir is Dyraheio, a picturesque expanse of high mountains which is Rogaland's equivalent of the southern Hardangervidda. It is a dramatic mountain landscape with a number of marked peaks, the highest of which is Snønut at 1606 metres above sea level. Reindeer live here, in larger numbers than anywhere else in Rogaland, and the area has good trout fishing too. Signs of pollution are fewer than further south.

The Stavanger Touring Association's network of marked trails, with cabins at regular intervals, makes these areas accessible summer and winter.

Old outfarms – *støl* – abound in the highlands, some of them much modernised but others still rejoicing in age old sympathy between nature and man. Hamrabøheia is a prime example of this: the mountain farms between Suldalsvatnet, Skaulen and Hylsfjord must be among the loveliest in Rogaland.

The county's northernmost valley is Kvanndalen, which stretches towards Haukelifjell and the Hardangervidda. Along its path it touches the skirts of the 1656 metre high Vassdalseggen, the county's tallest peak. Just west of here is Breifonn, almost as high, and the only glacier in Rogaland.

Above: In the heart of the mountains, at Vormedalsheia overlooking the Bokna-fjord, in the municipality of Hjelmeland.
Photograph: Kjell Helle Olsen

Below: Enveloped in a patina of tradi-tion, one of the mountain outfarms in the Ryfylke which are used for summer grazing. This one at Vormedalsheia.
Photograph: Kjell Helle Olsen

On the rooftop of Rogaland, atop the 1606 m. peak of Snønuten at Dyraheio in Suldal.
Photograph: Per Frøyland Pallesen.

The herd of reindeer at bottom proves Dyraheio has been aptly named: in Norwegian the name means "deer hills".
Photograph: Kjell Helle Olsen.

On the opposite page: Rogaland's only glacier.
Photograph: Per Frøyland Pallesen.

One hundred years of life in the mountains

The picture below is from an excursion to Nilsebu in the summer of 1987, during the celebration of the Stavanger Touring Association's 100th anniversary. The exact date was earlier, marked with a celebration at the Stavanger Konserthus which included an exhibition of Rogaland nature photographs.

The Stavanger Touring Association has contributed greatly to local enjoyment of life in the open, making nature accessible to thousands who would not venture forth without the safety of the marked paths and overnight lodges. The association's yearbooks are an eagerly awaited yearly event.

Photograph: Egil Eriksson.

From Utsira to Olalia

North Rogaland's landscape is also typical of the west coast, but in a different way from the Ryfylke. The outer coast is low lying and rugged, with a chopped-up appearance. The rocks here originate from the core of the caledonian mountain chain formation, and are volcanic. They are hard, and divided into many different types. The landscape is crisscrossed with fault lines which the many fjords and sounds follow, mostly in a north/south direction, and at right angles to the path eroded by the inland ice. Because of this, the depths and heights are less predominant than towards the inner Ryfylke.

The island of Utsira sits like a solitary outpost in the North Sea, some twenty kilometres beyond the rest of the coastline. It is unprotected by skerries or beaches and at the mercy of thundering waves which have eroded these coastal cliffs – both here and on the western side of Karmøy – into remarkable formations.

Immediately behind this wild coastal strip is fertile agricultural land, sheltered by a low ridge. This combination of North Sea outpost and sheltered vegetation has made Utsira into a place visited by a great variety of birds, some of them rare. Utisra is internationally renown among ornithologists.

The fulmar petrel is one of the rarer species to be seen at this marine reserve.   *Photograph: Per Frøyland Pallesen*

The smaller islands between Utsira and Karmøy are also attractive to seabirds; Spannholmene, Urter, Ferkningstadsøyene and a few others are seabird cliffs. These islands are a riot of colour with the flowers of early summer.

Karmøy is a combination of the natural and the man-imposed. Man's influence can be seen on much of the island, in coniferous plantations among others. Much of Karmøy's original character has been lost through development, but traces do remain. Outstanding is the area surrounding the Avaldsnes Church, which at one time was Harald Hårfagre's royal estate.

Karmøy, Bokn and western Tysvær are mainly heath country with an abundance of common heather as well as bell and purple heather, which transform the bleakness into a blaze of colour in August. Deciduous trees appear towards Haugaland to the east, where they live intermixed with the heather. This was a forested area in earlier days and it appears that, with reduced grazing, the woods are returning.

Haugesund, Tysvær and Bokn are full of variation, with elevations providing good views over the otherwise flat landscape. Boknafjell is particularly interesting and the Haugesund hills provide distant views and good hiking in sheltered woods. The Tysvær woods are even better protected from the western winds. The wooded sections along the beaches are fine recreation areas. Natural pine woods extend from Skjoldafjord towards Boknafjord in the east. The best description of this landscape is through the paintings of Rogaland's famous Lars Hertevig.

North Rogaland coast.   *Photograph: Tor Brekke*

Lars Hertevig's "Borgøya". The island of Borgøya is in the Hervikfjord in Tysvær.

The forests of Tysvær and Vindafjord and the northern part of the Ryfylke have increasing colonies of moose and roe deer, while those in the southern part of the country are abundant in the smaller red deer. Thus, all four kinds of Norwegian deer are represented in Rogaland. As the animal population increases, so does the popularity of hunting in Rogaland.

From Vindafjord towards the west the landscape is reminiscent of the Ryfylke.

The inner areas are more gentle, with moraine covered slopes topped by mountain peaks, and with broad and fertile valleys such as the Vikedal.

Through the valley flows the Vikedal river in lazy curves, interrupted only by short stretches with falls and rapids. This is a good salmon river and the falls of Lokafossen are well worth of visit.

The highlands north of Vikedal are one of Rogaland's finest ski areas, with Olalia as the geographical centre. This region represents nature with a wild flavour are its best, summer and winter. Around Sauda and Hordaland bears have been seen now and then, wolverines live in the highlands of Rogaland, and even lynx in the more inaccessible valleys. Of all the Norwegian beasts of prey, only the wolf is missing in Rogaland. Surely, this is a many faceted county, with samples of most of what Norwegian nature has to offer, but on a mere three percent of the country's total surface.

Rogalanders don't know their county well enough. They don't know about the variety and depth of experience available to them within a short journey. Nature in Rogaland is a bountiful source of outdoors life and tourism which could be taken advantage of to far greater degree than it is today.

Hills of heather: The melancholy beauty of summer's approaching end.

Of all the deer species, it is the roe deer that is the most adaptable, not seeming to mind the intrusion of man into his territory. Photograph: Rune Roaldkvam

The North Sea thunders as we fly over the Røværsholm lighthouse at Haugesund. On a day such as this one, there is good visibility and a fresh northwester.
Photograph: Tor Brekke

They call the puffin a "sea-parrot" along the coast. Photograph: Rune Roaldkvam

Rogaland and the Rogalanders

By: Lars Vaage

Rogaland was one of the first areas in Norway to be settled. Presumably these first settlers came from other North Sea countries some 12,000 years ago, since at that time most of the North Sea was dry land, with only the Norwegian Gut between them and Rogaland. The oldest trace of habitation that we are certain about is some 11,000 years old. The cave dwelling at Vistehola was lived in about 8900 years ago, and the first drowning of a Rogalander that we know about happened at this time too, in Breivik north of Haugesund.

The climate in those days was mild and the land was covered with dense forests. Because of the large quantity of ice that had pressed down upon the land for millenia, the North Sea penetrated further into the country than it does now. Small elevations in the landscape used to be islands or peninsulas, with sheltered bays and sounds in between. We have been left with place names that appear unreasonable to us today: names that end in "a" which, according to some scientists, used to mean island (øy) such as Sola, Madla, Hinna, Goa, Joa, etc. – all of them firmly part of the mainland today.

The South-Westland, with Rogaland in its centre, was

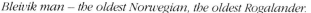

Bleivik man – the oldest Norwegian, the oldest Rogalander.

Huge bones were uncovered while digging in a cellar in Finnøy. The Stavanger Archaeological Museum was alerted and they promptly went to work: to find the better part of the skeleton of a polar bear who met his death all of 10,000 years ago.
Photograph: Ragne Johnsrud/Tveit

Re-enacting life in the Bronze Age. The bronze "lur" were found at Revheim in Stavanger, and are thought to have been used in connection with religious ceremonies. The lur are believed to have been made in Rogaland.

the site of some of the earliest large settlements in Norway, ruled by powerful clans of chieftains from North Jæren and the area around Karmsund. This is problably the reason why the first king of Norway, Harald Hårfagre, needed to subjugate all the other regions before he dared to tackle the South-Westland. The decisive battle against his last significant opponent took place at Hafrsfjord, near Stavanger, towards the end of the 800s, probably in the late summer of 872. The outcome of this battle – which the Rogalanders lost – was that Norway was united for the first time in one kingdom, under one king.

Rogalanders and the kingdom's authorities

Ever since then, however, Rogalanders have had a tendency to view the central government with a degree of skepticism. With good reason, too, since this central government has always extracted greater goods from the county than the value of what they have given in return.

In any event, King Harald thought it wisest to keep the recalcitrant Rogalanders under constant supervision. He settled in Rogaland with his occupation forces for the rest of his life.

Thus, Norway's first "capital" was at Utstein, in Rennesøy municapality. We know this because a contemporary skald, Thorbjørn Hornklove, in his famous epic about the victory at Hafrsfjord refers to: ". . . The mighty king, who lives at Utstein. . . ". Later he moved to the royal residence at Alvaldsnes on Karmøy and after his death he was buried at Haugalandet, where a memorial was raised to him on Haraldshaugen in 1872.

Will not bow

Even in those days some Rogalanders could not find it in themselves to bow to the king of the nation. Instead, many sailed west to live in freedom on the islands out there. Eirik Raude was one of these. He eventually reached Greenland and his son, Leiv Eriksson, became the first known European discoverer of America.

A hundred years after the reign of Harald, Rogaland's most famous chieftain, Erling Skjalgson, crossed the country from Sognefjord to Rygjarbit on the Southland coast. Skjalgson's wife Astrid was the king's sister and it is said of him that he gave his serfs land to cultivate, so they could work themselves to freedom. Because of this, he is called

Norway's first real social politician. He was so powerful that the future king, Olav Haraldsson, attempted to have Erling killed; which cost the king his life and his kingdom. However, it was this which in turn lead to King Olav becoming Saint Olav, Norway's Eternal King. The results of our actions are often unforseen.

In the 1120s Stavanger became a bishopric and soon after that construction began on St. Svithun's Cathedral dedicated to the patron saint of Winchester in England. This was logical, since the first Christian influence to coastal Norway came mainly from England. The first bishop, Reinald, was an Englishman. Reinald was eventually hanged because he refused to hand over the bishopric's wealth to the King of the nation, Harald Gille.

Norway's only medieval cathedral

The Cathedral was built, rebuilt and extended in the course of a couple of hundred years, in a combination of romanesque and gothic. It is the only medieval cathedral in Norway which has been in constant use until our own times. There it stands, in the centre of the city's and the county's pulsating life.

The last "prime minister" in Norway before the union with Denmark – the local ruler Ogmund Finson from Hesby on Finnøy — was a Rogalander. His death ushered in the long, dark centuries in Rogaland's history.

Jewels from the early Viking Age, found at Gausel in Stavanger.

Artist's impression of life in the Iron Age at Forsandmoen in the Ryfylke fjords. 　　　　　　　　　　*Water colour: Else Lauvanger.*

The oldest Rogalanders were hunters, but as long as 5000 years ago they had acquired their first domestic animals – cows, sheep and goats. Fishing was certinly practised from time to time by even the earliest inhabitants. Gradually, they also took up working the soil. The oldest grain of corn found in Norway – 4000 years old – was discovered under what is now Sola airport.

Gateway to Europe
North Jæren and the outer Ryfylke islands had good soil and sold grain to other parts of the country. Rogalanders became good craftsmen early on, making their own tools and ornaments. They became traders, exchanging goods with other countries. Rogaland has always been one of this country's gateways to Europe.

Also, our ancestors were in no way as primitive as we like to imagine; a beautifully decorated 3000 year old bronze shaving knife which was found at Sola shows that they were not necessarily the bearded brigands often pictured. Remember too that northerners are the only race who have set aside a whole day in the week for bathing and washing – *laugadag* (lørdag): Saturday.

A free and independent people they were. The tendency to be at odds with the national government seemed to crop up fairly often. In 1591 King Christian II – Christian the Tyrant – raised taxes by 10% on all goods in order to finance his campaigns against Sweden. Large parts of Rogaland refused to pay this tax, with the result that they were levied a hefty fine two years later, at the same time as Rogaland's chief, Orm Eriksson, was hanged by the authorities. A later tax strike was more sucessful: in 1760 it was the farmers who won their point and the king, county administrator and bailiff who had to give in.

Logs to Amsterdam
Around the 1500s forestry was a major source of income, in addition to the traditional ones of agriculture, fisheries, crafts and trading. It is said that parts of London and of Amsterdam are built upon Rogaland timber. This, however, led to deforestation in the county, the effects of which are still to be seen.

In 1682 King Christian V moved the bishopric and the office of the King's representative to the new town he had built, and which he had named after himself: Kristiansand. This was a hard blow for the whole county of Rogaland, affecting it throughout the next two centuries.

Farmers and fishermen
Day to day life for the Rogalander was a struggle more often than not. Most were farmers but on the islands, particularly in the Karmsund area, fishing was also important. In the late 1800s Stavanger became the second largest port in Norway,

The interior of the reconstructed Iron Age Farm at Ullandhaug in Stavanger.　　　　*Photograph: Ragne Johnsrud*

and Haugesund was established as the centre for herring fishing and export. Towards the end of the 1800s, in the transition from sail to steamships, Stavanger's ship owners lagged behind. Gradually the canning industry took over as Stavanger's principal livelihood. This was around the time that the saying was born about Stavanger being built on "fish and ships", while Haugesund was built on herring bones.

Times were prosperous for Rogaland from the middle of the 1800s right up until 1920. The population increased sharply and Rogaland grew in these years from a farming and fishing county into an industrial one, the majority of the population living in towns and urban areas.

Industry grows

In Sandnes a new town grew up around the brick works. Egersund started a pottery factory whose products can be admired today at the Pottery Museum. Rogaland is one of the county's biggest sheep counties and, in order to make use of the wool, large spinneries were established at Ålgård, Sandnes, Stavanger and Oltedal. Copper ore was found at Karmøy and the mines at Vistnes were for a long time one of the county's major industries. The mines gained international fame in 1986 when it was proved that the copper facing of the Statue of Liberty in New York came mostly from the Vistnes mines.

Hydroelectric power was first harnessed in the early 1900s and led to the development of industrial plants such as the one at Sauda and at Jørpeland. At present, Rogaland is one of the counties with the most extensive hydroelectric power development. In the Ryfylke highlands we have one

of Norway's largest man-made lakes, the Blåsjø reservoir. The first major gas power station in Norway is to be built in Rogaland in the near future.

The cannery era

The predominant livelihood of this century were canning and herring fisheries; these two made up for about 80% of Stavanger's total industry in the 1930s. At times the smell of herring oil hung low over the towns of Haugesund, Stavanger and Egersund. "Smells like money", people used to say with satisfaction.

Meanwhile, on Jæren, agriculture was developing. Plows from Kverneland are found today over the entire world. The facilitator for this development was transportation: the Jæren railway opened in 1878 and boat connections were increased, both in the Ryfylke fjords and to other parts of the country. (Con'd. pg. 62)

Re-production of a woman's outfit from the Migratory Age around 400-600.

The picture on this page is by Ragne Johnsrud. It shows an view of the Ullandhaug Iron Age farm, where it is easy to imagine one self transported 14-15 centuries back in time.
Photograph: Ragne Johnsrud

Iron Age farm at Ullandhaug

The Iron Age farm at Ullandhaug is a popular tourist attraction. A whole farm complex has been recreated on foundations discovered during archaelogical excavations. The new farmhouses were built under museum supervision, in the same style and with the same materials, tools and techniques available to the original builders: Iron Age man.

In the tourist season there are guided tours by museum staff and demonstrations of cooking, spinning and weaving, as they were practised here some thousand years ago.

Place of destiny

After two years of circling the globe, Ragnar Thorseth sailed into Hafrsfjord on the "Saga Siglar", the fjord where Norway became united into one kingdom. It is here that Harald Hårfagre – Fairhair – won his final battle against the many small rulers of the land in the year 872. The symbol of this united kingdom, Harald's memorial stone, stands in Haugesund where it was raised in 1872, for the millenium of the foundation of the nation.

Yet another memorial to the union, the Three Swords, were erected at Hafrsfjord in 1983.

Rogaland is still one of our most important agricultural areas. A major part of Norway's meat, milk, cheese, chicken, egg and vegetable production come from here. The soil on Jæren is good, but extremely rocky. The miles-long stone walls bear witness to this, and to the struggle that went into clearing the Jæren soil for farming. The Ryfylke area, on the other hand, has concentrated on fruit growing and greenhouses.

Natural fertilizer from Bergen played an important role in this agricultural development. Freighters regularly shuttled between Bergen and Stavanger, bringing the contents of the Bergen privies, to the benefit of Jæren farms.

The ones who left
The emigration from Norway to America was spurred by powerful social reasons. However, the first group who set out from Stavanger harbour on July 4, 1825 in a little sloop called "Restauration", left in quest of freedom; the freedom to worship God in their own way. Christianity's roots grew firmly in Rogaland. It is no coincidence that the Norwegian Missionary Society or the Norwegian Teetotalitarian Society were founded in Stavanger. This was also the home of the preacher Lars Oftedal, one of the country's great social thinkers and innovators.

A woman of importance was buried at a gravemound in Klepp around the year 400. 500 years later a stone cross was erected at the site, as a symbol of the "White Christ", whose teachings had come to this land.   *Photograph: Ragne Johnsrud*

It is not a coincidence that the main figure behind the introduction of decentralisation in government in Norway in 1837, Ole Gabriel Ueland, was a Rogalander. Sadly, much of the work he started remains unfinished; petty bureaucrats of the central government still cling to many of the positions of power here in Norway, as elsewhere.

A practial people
Rogalanders are known for being practical. A good illustration of this is the tall marker stone called "the Virgin Mary's sewing needle", which stands leaning towards the church at Avaldsnes, on Karmøy. It is said that on the day when the tip of the stone touches the wall of the church, the world will come to an end and Judgement Day will be upon us. However, it is also said that in the dark of night, the Avaldsnes Church priests now and then venture forth, to chip bits off the tip of the stone.

World War II came to Rogaland on the morning of April 9, 1940. The name of Stavanger airport, Sola, has been firmly inscribed in the history of that war, as the airport was occupied under the first parachute attack in history. Some of the hardest battles of the ensuing days were fought at Gloppedalen, a valley filled by one of the greatest rock falls in northern Europe.

Thanks to the enormous strategic importance of the Stavanger airport at Sola and of the Stavanger harbour, this district was one of the most tightly guarded during the war. When the German occupational forces lay down their arms on May 7, 1945, the relief and gratitude felt in Rogaland was enormous – as it was in the entire country.

Oil is discovered
By the 1960s both the canning industry and shipping had had their day, and the county faced hard times. It was then that the oil industry stepped in. Stavanger immediately realised the potential and lost no time in creating an environment conducive to making Stavanger the natural choice for the oil capital of Norway. This was the necessary spark for the almost fairy tale development of both city and county. In the course of a few short years we have moved from being a city and a county of humble means, to having some of the nation's wealthiest population and some of the wealthiest municipalities. The oil industry put into motion a rarely seen rise in the standard of living.

Rogalanders from the southern part of Boknafjord have long been known for their knack for understatement. In olden days, the modest Siddis would say "I am from Stavanger, does it matter?" Nowadays this has changed into "I am from Stavanger, what of it?"

Olavskirken, Olav's Church, at Avaldsnes has a medieval nave and choir. The church was begun under orders of King Håkon Håkonsen, who however did not live to see it finished. Photograph: AmS
Built much later, one of Rogaland's finest churches: the Jelsa Church.   *Photograph: Inge Bruland*

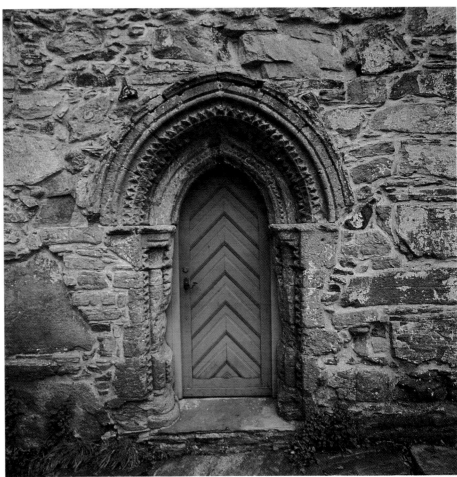

Utstein Kloster

King Magnus Lagabøter, the Lawmaker, founded Utstein Abbey, on the island of Utstein in the Ryfylke fjord around the year 1200. After the Reformation, the farms belonging to the abbey came into private ownership. Eventually the old buildings fell into disrepair.

Architect Gerhard Fischer led a major restoration project and today Utstein Kloster is a living museum. One of the buildings has been furnished with small bedrooms in order to make it suitable for seminars.

Ustein Kloster is one of Norway's best preserved abbeys. It is a popular tourist attraction where the historical riches of the atmosphere is quickly sensed.

The photograph to the left is taken by Ragne Johnsrud, the other two are by Johnsrud/Tveit.

Stavanger Cathedral

Stavanger was no more than a small settlement at the tip of *Vågen*, the harbour, when the building of the Cathedral was undertaken around the year 1100. It is as impressive as the many other, much larger cathedrals which were built in the middle ages.

Right next to it is the Cathedral School, *Stavanger Katedralskole*, now a senior high school no longer associated with the church.

Stavanger became a bishopric because it was the only populated area along the southwest coast. The Cathedral was originally built as a romanes-

que basilica, in anglo-norman style. It was almost totally destroyed by a huge fire in 1272 and was rebuilt by Bishop Arne with a larger, gothic choir.

After the Reformation, the Danish rulers laid claim to the wealth of the church and even the bells of Stavanger Cathedral were removed and sent to Copenhagen. The ship, with bells on board, sank along the coast of Jæren and, according to legend, at times of storm their peal can still be heard in the vicinity.

Photographs: Ellingsen

The good life

Two grand Stavanger-houses have been carefully preserved. They show the lifestyle of the wealthy some generations back when the difference between rich and poor was vast. All the same, the difference does not appear to have bred envy or indignation among the poor over social injustice. Rather, it may have served to feed the workers' imagination with dreams of riches and rewards to come in the afterlife. Their faith assured them that their place in life was the will of God.

Ledaal was built for the Kielland family in 1800. It is now Stavanger's royal residence and is used by the municipality for formal receptions. The house is open to the public. The picture to the left was taken when the Stavanger Museum held open house. What more appropriate than visitors wearing costumes in keeping with the environment?

The villa at Breidablikk, above, was built in the 1880s by a wealthy businessman and it is preserved in the style of one hundred years ago, both inside and out. Breidablikk has been willed to a foundation, which looks after it.

Photographs: Ove Dahlstrøm.

Shipping and canning

Canning, as an industry, has come to an end in Stavanger. Most of the town's fleet is sailing under other nation's flags. Thus, it is all the more welcome that the memories of the time when ships from Stavanger crossed the oceans of the world, are kept alive.

In two of Stavanger's old sea-houses, painstakingly restored, we now find the Stavanger Maritime Museum and the Merchant Museum. In Øvre Strandgate stands the the Canning Museum (lower left). The restoration of the two sea-houses earned Stavanger the Europa Nostra Prize and an extra feather in the hat of Einar Hedén, the man responsible for the preservation of *Gamle Stavanger,* the old town.

The picture at top right shows the shipowner's office, now reassembled a the Maritime Museum and looking much as it did a hundred years ago. At top left we are given a glance inside a shipowner's home. Below, the Merchant Museum, where an old general store has been reconstructed down to the last detail. Bottom right: the sailmakers' loft.

Photographs: Dag M. Søiland.

A grand gift

Leif Østby, in his book on Norwegian culture, mentions the classical trend in Norwegian architecture in the 20s. He calls the Haugesund Town Hall one of this trend's most significant examples. The Town Hall was given to Haugesund by the shipowner Knut Knutsen O.A.S. and his wife Elisabeth Bakke. The building was inaugurated on October 1, 1931 and the Town Hall Square on August 28, 1949. It was eventually landscaped thanks to a donation from the now widowed Elisabeth and the Knutsen family. On the following page, The Three Swords, by sculptor Fritz Røed, impaled on the shores of Hafrsfjord in Stavanger.
Photograph: Inge Bruland.

Culture

By: Lars Chr. Sande

When the 100th anniversary of the theatre in Stavanger was celebrated in 1983, it was with the performance of *"Læraren"* – The Teacher – by Arne Garborg. Ivar Nørve played the part of Paulos Hove. Hove's religious scruples have been looked upon as fairly typical for the coast of Rogaland – labelled the Dark Mainland during the heated cultural debates of the 1800s. And dark it must have been inside the mind of the teacher, with all his anxious faith. Still, it is no less dark in the mind of Hamlet as he wanders around the graveyard with a skull in his hand, posing the all important question about being, or not. Hamlet, Shakespeare's greatest drama, was played at Rogaland Theatre in the autumn of 1986, for an audience numbering some 10.000 people. Darkness of the soul was not relieved when the director of the theatre, Bentein Baardson, raised the curtain around the new year of 1987 on Dostoevski's Brothers Karamazov with their debates about the existence of God.

Jan Grønli as Hamlet.

Ivar Norve in "Læraren".

Still, the public seems not to be frightened away by such soul searching seriousness; yet another 10.000 viewers filled the theatre before the final performance was over.

Swinging Stavanger

The pendulum did eventually swing towards lighthearted fun: *"Johanna og Broremann"*, full of Stavanger ballads with lyrics by the city's favorite native writer, Andreas Jacobsen, warmed many a soul and box office queues were long. Including the performances at the large capacity Concert House, close to 35.000 people – a record – got to see Johanna and her little brother flying through Stavanger history on wings of music.

There was more to Rogaland Theatre's repertoire during this especially active season: "Rottefangeren", a family show written by Morten Jorstad, gave the young actors of the Children's Theatre a chance to test their talents alongside the adults. It was an exciting, and touching, first performance for this musical – which also attracted full houses.

The actors of Johanne og Broremann: Ketil Egge, Sally Nilsen, Gretelill Tangen, Mia Gundersen, Dag Schreiner, Per Inge Torkelsen, Thor Inge Kristiansen.

Next page: a scene in "Rottefangeren" with Ketil Høgh in the main role.

Haugesund is eager to catch up with Stavanger. The Haugesund Theatre was opened during the spring of 1987 with much festivity and a great children's show.

Amanda from Haugesund

Haugesund has always been eager to make a name for itself with in the cultural image of Rogaland. *Haugesundrevyen* – The Haugesund variety show – has been responsible for much entertainment. However, what people comment on most of all these days is that Haugesund is about to become the headquarters of the Norwegian Film Festival and the Amanda Prize Awards ceremony. The prize, by the way, owes its name to the buxom "Amanda from Haugesund" celebrated far and wide in song for her charm and her warmth and, above all, for her delightful plumpness. The generosity of Amanda's figure is reproduced in a statue, and in the miniatures which are the Amanda awards.

As one of the elite of the film industry, Liv Ullmann has been enticed to the Haugesund film festival. Along with her come other well know movie personalities. No wonder that for a few super-active days Haugesund feels very much part of the big world.

Stavanger Festival Days

Festival Days were arranged in Stavanger in 1983 and again in 1985. In 1986 it was the turn of the Emigration Festival – Roots 86. These cultural events attracted world class artists to the city. Stavanger Festival Days gave impetus to the building of the new Concert House, and the transformation of Bjergsted into a music park. It was a year laden with optimism and plenty of tax revenues when a Kulturhus – cultural centre – was embarked upon at both Sola and Stavanger, while Haugesund established its Festival. In Gjesdal a large covered amphitheathre capable of seating an audience of 3000 was built at the new Kongeparken amusement park, and in Stavanger the Sportshall was furnished with seats and a stage for holding big attractions.

Joint effort

Long before these large public constructions were undertaken, a number of private groups or local organizations were doing their utmost to raise a community hall or a place of religious gathering. There is not another county in Norway that can point to such a measure of community spirit. This is where the true traditions lie: it was after a

(Con'd. pg. 80)

No one comes closer to the heart of Stavanger than Andreas Jacobsen, alias Ajax. His dramatised stories have broken one box office record after the other at Rogaland Theatre. It was a great honour when this well loved author visited a class at the Mosterøy school.

Film festival

Liv Ullmann has become a patron of the Haugesund Film Festival. She comes to Rogaland with pleasure, this is where her career was launched-playing the part of Anne Frank at the Rogaland Theatre in 1956. She returned to Stavanger during the Festival Days in 1983, playing Anne Frank at the theatre again, 25 years later. In the picture to the right, she is receiving the "Spreader of Joy" award from the hands of Haugesund mayor, Edvard Ringen.

Photograph: Erik Østberg.

At the top of the page: the theatre building in Haugesund.

Photograph: Tor Brekke.

revival meeting conducted by the near legendary preacher, Lars Oftedal in the 1800s that prayer halls started springing up around the county like mushrooms. Bethania, for example, was built in Stavanger as the city's largest meeting hall, one of the largest in Norway in fact, with a capacity of 3000 closely packed souls.

What with houses built by community effort, plus a variety of halls, concert hall and cultural centre, Rogaland is well equipped for cultural growth in the years to come.

Musical quickening

The establishment of Rogaland Theatre as a permanent institution in Stavanger was an important cultural milestone in the '50s. Yet another important step was taken around 1970, when the Stavanger Ensemble was replaced by the Stavanger Radio Orchestra – which in those days needed to reach to eastern Europe, particularly Czechoslovakia, to find musicians for string instruments. This flourishing radio and symphony orchestra created important side effects: a Czechoslovakian musician, Petr Cejka, took it upon himself to found the Stavanger Symphony Choir. Under his sure leadership and together with the orchestra, the choir has achieved a number of musical successes. *(Cont'd. pg. 84)*

Young talent

The musical life of Rogaland blooms in so many ways, not least in the emergence of promising young talent, trained and encouraged by top local teachers.

Music schools exist in a number of municipalities; colleges offer music courses and the Rogaland Music Conservatorium it noteworthy. The pictures on these two pages show first rate Rogaland talents. On this page it is Truls Otterbech Mørch on tour with his cello in New York. He took part in a concert in Stavanger in the spring of 1987 together with the singer Malmfrid Sand, trumpet player Ole Andersen and tuba player Mads Bryne who, in spite of his youth, has won a number of awards. From England came Rod Franks with his trumpet. Bjørn Woll conducted. In the foreground stands Leif Ove Andsnes, 18, from Karmøy, a highly promising pianist who has won among others, the Hindemith prize.

Photograph: Finn Refvem.

Music Park

Brahms' German Requiem was on the programme when this photograph of the Stavanger Symphony Orchestra was taken. Ever since the Concert House was opened in 1983 it has seen much activity. The auditorium can seat some 1100 listeners.

There is also a smaller building at Bjergsted, the Music House, which contains the Rogaland Music Conservatorium and furnishes the Symphony Orchestra with rooms. In addition, the park has a hall for amateurs adjoining the administration wing, and rooms for the Stavanger Music

School. The painted glass windows of the Music House was done by the internationally acclaimed Stavanger artist, Kjell Pahr Iversen. Photograph: Dag Magne Søyland.

The painter who wants to be an angel of light

Stavanger painter Kjell Pahr-Iversen has said about himself that he would like to be an angel of light. His paintings glow.

Pahr-Iversen has exhibited in a number of countries, among them the United States and France. His work has received international acclaim.

Photograph: Jonas Friestad.

Local fashion designers

The last word in Stavanger fashion, modelled against the old houses along Stra'en, by their creators.

Left: Åse Sandvik Tendenes in pastels, Charlotte Zink in the two piece, and Gitte Andersen in "Grace Jones" hood and her version of the little black dress. Photograph: Jonas Friestad

Atlantis at the "Atlantic"

Atlantis was a legendary island west of Europe. Plato tells us – based on Egyptian sources – that Atlantis sank in the deep, overnight. Its culture is said to have been highly advanced and they ruled over some

of the western mediterranean countries as well. This fabled island has been the subject of much speculation, here indulged in by the painter Ole Nesvik on ten floors of the Atlantic Hotel in Stavanger. Here we have six of the paintings based on the tragedy that befell this paradise. The question is, has Atlantis ever existed, or does it belong to the world of metaphysics, a collective memory of a paradise that has been lost, but will be regained? Ole Nesvik was born and educated in Stavanger and lived in his native town during the early part of his artistic career. He now lives at the Ekely artists' commune in Oslo.

Culture House on Sølvberget

For over 50 years plans for Sølvberget were discussed in Stavanger. It seemed to be a difficult municipal nut to crack. But now there stands the Culture House, with its six storeys and 11,000 square metres of floor space and a final price tag of around 250 million kroner. The building is home to a library, numerous cinemas, activity centers and tempting shops of artistic interest.

Responsible for this building is architect Kjell Lund, the man who also designed Norway's most expensive building: the new Norges Bank. Lund was determined that the Culture House should not clash with its surroundings in Old Stavanger. He appears to have been successful in this.
Photograph: Jonas Friestad.

Yet another Czechoslovakian musician joined the orchestra: Frantisek Veselka who has since become a sought after violin teacher at the Rogaland Music Consevatorium.

The sound of brass bands

Rogaland is outstanding for its band music, particularly in the North Jæren district. The Stavanger Brass Band has won several Norwegian championships and won points at major European competitions. In fact, the band has been Scandinavian Champion.

Close contact with the traditionally popular British brass bands has brought a number of conductors and performers to Stavanger, where many a successful nationwide band music competition has been held.

Visible on the map of Norway

Writers and poets such as Alexander Kielland and Arne Garborg have ensured a place for Rogaland in the literature of Norway. Both men gathered much of their material from conditions they saw in Rogaland. So did Alfred Hauge, who died in the autumn of 1986; he observed the world from a Ryfylke landscape, from Sjernarøyane to be exact, the home of his childhood. He was keenly interested in the emigration from Rogaland to America and wrote a trilogy about Cleng Peerson, a figure with whom Hauge felt a strong identification.

With 12-tone music

If we are to pin-point Rogaland's contribution to the music of the nation, two men come instantly to mind: Sparre Olsen

who was born in Stavanger but moved early from the town, and Fartein Valen whose family – missionaries – were from Stavanger. The 100th anniversary of the birth of Valen – who went to school in Stavanger – was celebrated with a memorial concert at the Stavanger Concert House in the autumn of 1987.

Painter of light

Lars Hertevig was doomed to wander in darkness for many years. However, before his brilliant artistic talent was extinguished by insanity, he created masterpieces of Norwegian painting. Even when suffering from his afflication, this son of Quakers from Tysvær managed to capture the quality of light better than most other Norwegian painters.

Nature has always been an important source of inspiration to Rogaland painters, particularly the light of Jæren, where to changing skies create endless variation.

The Stavanger Permanent Collection is planning to build a museum of art at Mosvann Park. The Stavanger Art Association is a focal point in the local art world and the *Bildende Kunstnernes Forening* – the painter's association – supports its members by arranging exhibitions and promoting sales.

Stavanger the mission town

The Norwegian Mission Company was founded in 1842 in Stavanger and sent its first missionaries to South Africa and Madagascar, later to other countries as well. At home in Norway, the company raised funds by arranging lecture tours for missionaries on leave, to tell about their experiences.

The meeting hall revolution

Mission county

Well over a hundred years ago the Stavanger preacher and newspaperman Lars Oftedal laid the foundations for what was to become an extensive network of religious meeting halls. According to the calculations of the Stavanger Aftenblad, some 10.000 square metres of meeting hall have been built just in the counties of Gjesdal, Klepp, Time and Hå. Much of the construction has been done on a voluntary basis, by community effort. Our hard workers are photographed on the roof of a new meeting hall at Lye field, a new residential development on Jæren. They are Arnfinn Vigrestad, Brynjulf Ausstad and Ivar Slettebø.

Photograph: Geir Sveen.

The Norwegian Missionary Society was founded in 1842 in Stavanger. The first missionaries went to South Africa and eventually intensive mission work was established on the island of Madagascar. Today the Missionary Society, with its headquarters in Stavanger, has operations in twelve countries, on four continents.

Funding comes from 5600 local mission groups over the entire country. Missionaries are trained in Stavanger.

The photographs on the opposite page show the School of Mission and Theology with old and new buildings. Three of the students studying the societies extensive archives, and Rev. Hans Austnaberg from Karmøy christening a baby in Madagascar.

Photographs: Liv Helga L. Austnaberg and Jan B. Henriksen.

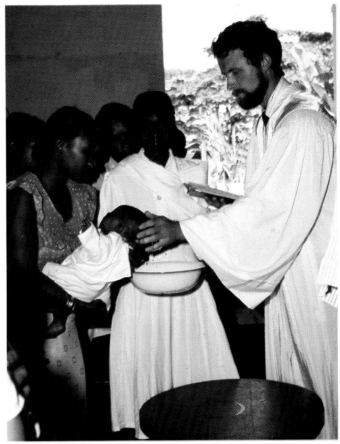

Revolution in education

In the course of its 13 years the *Høg-skolesenter* – college centre – of Rogaland, at Ullandhaug in Stavanger, has grown considerably. It is a visible proof of the revolution within the field of education.

Rogaland now trains civil engineers. Applicants can choose between a number of college level courses such as Norwegian, English, French, history, social studies and economy. The college complex is a hive of activity for some 2500 students and a faculty of 200.

The college centre is near Hafrsfjord. Here, seen from the air and facing northwest. In the foreground is the research libary, built thanks to a large donation by shipowner Sig. Bergesen d.y.

The college centre has also gained a fine aula recently, the 700-seat Tjodhallen.

Photograph: Tore T. Wiig.

Eigersund's Pottery Factory, 1884.

The pottery museum

Fayancemuseet – the pottery museum – in Eigersund was opened in 1986. Inside, examples of the 132 years of work of the town's potters are on view. On the opposite page, a lovely vase decorated by Th. Friestad. The factory specialised in inexpensive wares.

The Eigersund Pottery Museum is history come to life. It was a major local institution for 132 years, known far beyond the borders of Norway.

It was not even deemed necessary to advertise until the 1880s.

Eigersund Fayanse came into the limelight in 1898 at a national exhibition held in Bergen. The country's leading newspapers praised the products of the factory: "Here is functional and decorative pottery which stands up to the artistic standards of any foreign product in form, design and glazing".

Industry

By: Lars Chr. Sande

Two Norwegian Americans, one from Seattle and the other from Minneapolis, visited Stavanger in the summer of 1987. He was 65, she 25. They both had the same story to tell about their childhood, many years and miles apart.

They phoned the corner grocer. Did he happen to have King Oscar in a tin can? The helpful grocer answered yes, he did.

"Well, in that case, please let him out."

That is how much of a household word Kong Oscar Sardines – from Stavanger, Norway – were on the American market. And many Americans, not just the ones with Norwegian ancestors, consider the little fish from the clear Norwegian fjords at treat.

Stavanger still sends sardines to the U.S.A. Norway Foods, a conglomerate of the majority of Norwegian canneries including Chr. Bjelland& Co., has its headquarters in Stavanger. Their joint sales figure for 1986 was near 500 million Norwegian kroner. However, there are no longer any canneries in operation in Stavanger. The city whose fortunes rose or fell with that of the canneries – where endless rows of women stood, placing brisling sardines head to tail, head to tail, in tins by the thousands during the season – now looks to other sources of livelihood.

Canneries bring economic revival

It was the canning industry that revived Stavanger after the 1880 crash, when many of Stavanger's merchant houses went under due to the disappearance of herring from our shores, and the crisis in the shipping industry.

Haugesund did a fair amount of canning as well, right after the turn of the century.

If we look at the traditional industries of Rogaland, there are not many firms that date further than 100 years back. A couple of them, Jonas Øglænd and Kverneland A/S, have managed to sail through the changing times and continue at the helm of Rogaland's economy. Øglænd owns Scandinavia's largest bicycle factory, while Kverneland is the largest manufacturer of plows in the world.

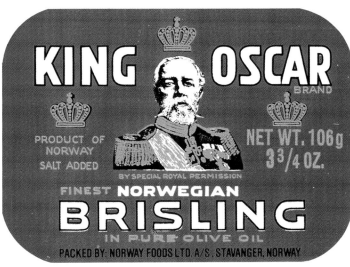

It is history

Once, brisling sardines used to be sent from Stavanger, on board the ships of the America Line. This picture of Strandkaien in Stavanger is from the early '60s. These days canned goods are sent to the United States via the continent. On the pallette being lifted aboard are 5850 cans of herring, exactly. To illustrate the size of the canning industry in Norway, it used to be said that a sardine was canned for every inhabitant of China.

Photograph: Nor-Hansen

Herring barrels in the foreground and fishing boats along the dock – a cliché of nostalgia of bygone herring days. For Haugesund, bygone by some 30 years in fact, although the barrels are still made there. The firm of Johannes Østensø prefers a factory in Jelsa where they make 280.000 herring barrels of plastic a year. But then, perhaps an empty plastic barrel serves just as well as an empty wooden one.
Photograph: Tor Brekke

Builders of wooden houses on deforested Jæren

It is almost a paradox that Block Watne, Norway's – and Scandinavia's – largest building manufacturer, should be located at Øksnevad, right in the middle of tree-less Jæren. The firm went in for prefabricated houses in the early 60s and has since expanded its range to cover a large variety in home design. The country's second largest building manufacturer, Hetlandshus, is also based at Jæren.

The battle against stone

The rocky landscape of Jæren was cleared with crowbar and a system of pulleys. Only recently has machinery been taken into use. The cultivation of Jæren has long been an honoured concept throughout Norway. Jæren farmers have always been highly ingenious and have succeeded in making the soil yield.

The density of cow population on Jæren is becoming the highest in the world, which is a boon to milk production but not for the waterways, which are becoming over ferti-

lised. The milk of Jæren is among the best in the world, and a large amount of it goes to make the world famous Jarlsberg cheese.

Further about the produce of Rogaland, see the chapter titled "Rogaland sets the table".

Proud shipbuilding traditions

A fully rigged schooner must be one of the loveliest sights the eye can behold. In 1879 one of the most elegant of ships that was built in Norway was launched in Hogganvik in the Ryfylke. "Særinmer" was her name and she was a marvellous example of Rogalanders' mastery of the noble art of shipbuilding.

But times change, and the future lay in steam engines. *Stavanger Støberi & Dok* built many steam ships, some for the route along our coast. Around the turn of the century their workshops were Rogaland's biggest employers. Number two on the list was Egersund's Pottery Factory, the *Egersund Fayancefabrikk.*

From ships to oil installations

Shipbuiding traditions were kept alive in Stavanger and in Haugesund. There was a time when *Haugesund Mekaniske Verksted* had an order for nine 30.000 tonners at one time. Stavanger's *Rosenberg Mekaniske Verksted* built a 16.000 tonne tanker right after the war, which was the largest in Norway at the time. They continued to break records, filling the orders of shipowner Sig. Begesen d.y. However, eventually the docks at Rosenberg yard were not large enough and Bergesen had to turn to Japan to have his supertankers built.

After a period building gas tankers, Rosenberg went over to supply the oil industry. *Kværner Brug* in Egersund did as well. The future of these huge concerns is now tied to the fate of oil development in the North Sea.

Agricultural cooperation

Rogaland's dynamic agriculture has crystallised in two major co-operatives: *Felleskjøpet Rogaland Agder* has a yearly turnover of 1,4 billion kroner and has branches at 12 locations in Rogaland and the two Agder counties, East and West.

Agro Fellesslakteri has a turnover of 1,6 billion kroner a year. They employ approximately 900 people and handle around 60% of all slaughtering in Rogaland and East and West Agder.

In addition, the *Rogaland Egglag* and *Gartnerhallen* – egg, vegetable and fruit co-ops – also do a large amount of business.

Ever more jobs

Service industries have increased sharply and there are more people employed in education than ever before. Rogaland county administration has 9000 people on its payroll, 6000 of them in the health sector.

Commerce has shown a sharp upward swing, reflecting the increased buying power of the Rogalander. The office jobs created by all the oil and related companies in the North Jæren district are also numerous. Whereas planners in the 1950s were allocating space for further heavy industry, now it is the so called intelligent industries which are being awarded building lots. The Forus area, between Stavanger, Sandnes and Sola, now has about 7000 work places, most of them in petroleum administration, clerical and sales jobs.

Power hungry industry

In the beginning of the century power stations were built for energy-dependent industries at Jørpeland and at Sauda. In 1967 the aluminium works at Karmøy started production, which has now been considerably expanded and been taken over wholly by Norsk Hydro.

If we just glance back at herring and brisling sardines as the basis for thousands of jobs, it seems almost incredible how Rogaland has emerged strengthened and revitalised from one economic crisis after the other.

The ups and down shipping

The shipping crisis in Rogaland started making its effect felt in the mid-70s. Shipyards could no longer depend on orders, traditional shipping lines were feeling the pinch and ever more vessels were being laid up in the fjords. In fact, about the only money to be made from ships was the fee charged for laying them up.

Both Norwegian and foreign vessels were laid up, as we see here in Bøvågen. The mainland of Karmøy is seen in the background. The picture was taken around 1983, when the number of laid up ships were at their peak. Then gradually they disappeared, one by one, to be chopped up, melted down or converted to other, more profitable uses. When it became apparent that the great tankers were no longer viable, many shipping companies went in for supply boats for the oil industry in the North Sea. Their success was enormous and new companies were formed seemingly overnight. All until the price of oil fell and exploration came practically to a standstill. This time it was the turn of the supply ships to be laid up, and many of their owners who went bankrupt.

Working the soil

Opposite: Torger Grude at Klepp still prefers to plow with a horse, although he is a rare sight. At Sørbø in Rennesøy tractors supply the energy at potato planting time.

Photograph: Jonas Friestad.

This page: Sheep herding is important to the economy of Rogaland farmers. Here we see the herd of Steinar Lima in Gjesdal, where little Jørgen Holt helps out. Average meat yield per animal is around 60 kilos a year.

Photograph: Pål Chistensen.

The good shepherd

It is said that Rogaland's attitude to religion has been influenced by this region's many similarities with the Holy Land: Rogalanders are used to guarding flocks of sheep just as in the land of Israel, and they are fishermen, as well. Jesper Ravndal from Gjesdal is seen here with his flock on his way down from the Sirdal mountains at the end of a summer of mountain grazing. Jesper is in his element in the midst of several thousand sheep peacefully munching, and the trusty coffee pot steaming in the open air.

The picture at bottom shows sheep being separated in Upper Sirdal. The rest of the journey downhill is made by truck. Rogaland has around 160.000

sheep over a year old. In a really good season there can be as many as 200.000.

Rogaland has Norway's highest sheep population.

Photograph: Guro Waksvik.

The most effective farming

Farmers in Eastern Norway have always the forests to fall back upon. Here on Jæren fortunes depend on what can be coaxed from the soil. Because of this, the Jæren farmer has become – by necessity – the most efficient in the nation. To the left is a well kept farm at Tu, by Frøylandsvatnet lake in Time. The barn above is at a farm in Varhaug. Photograph: Olav Garborg.

Below, we see milk turned into Jarlsberg cheese for export to the United States, at the Nærbø Meieri. The milk of Jæren is said to be among the world's finest.

Photograph: Pål Christensen.

Sandnes

Sandnes is known for making a go of things. First it was the clay industry with the raw material dug out of the lanes around the town. Then Jonas Øglænd, a local merchant, became interested in bicycles – which led to Scandinavia's largest bicycle factory at Kvål in Sandnes, employing 560 people. Øglænd has not departed from traditional marketing: its Cubus chain of moderately priced fashion shops had a turnover of 688 million kroner in 1986. Øglænd own 30 of the 130 shops in the chain. Another 200 employees at Øglænd make ready-to-wear clothes for the value of 82 millioner kroner a year, and yet other branches employ another 185 people. Total turnover for the Øglænd concern was 1,18 billion kroner in 1986.

Knitting wool is also spun at Sandnes. The names of Sandnes Ullvarefabrikk and Sandnes Kamgarn are well known to all knitters.

Then ther is Sjur Svaboe, who in the course of one year has been awarded three prizes for his *Hanabryggene* – the Hana wharves. The industrial work centre – photograph on this page – was awarded the *Byggeskikkprisen,* a building award, then NITO's technology prize, and then the municipality of Sandnes granted the new wharf buildings its Economy Prize. Svaboe shared the honours with the architects, Hoem, Kloster and Jacobsen.

80 people work at Hanabryggene, most of them on forward looking projects within computer technology, electronics and bio-technology. Svaboe's various business enterprises employ 2000 people, Scanvest Ring being the largest individual firm.

Yes, Sandnes is known for making a go of things.

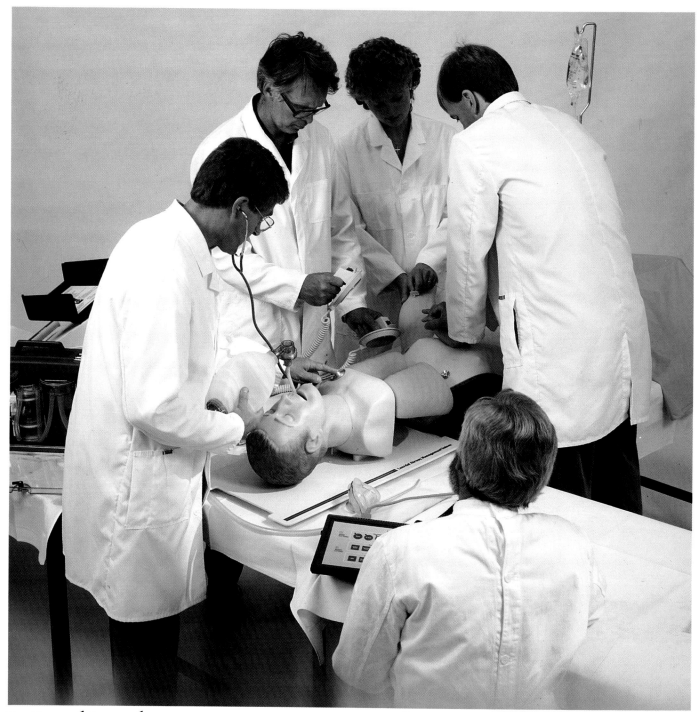

Medical equipment of world fame

Medical emergencies – and the equipment to handle them – are the key concepts at Laerdal Medical of Stavanger.

The big breakthrough for this Stavanger manufacturing firm was Resusci-Anne, the lifelike training doll used in the cardiopulmonary resuscitation technique CPR.

Over 20 million people have been trained in CPR with Resusci-Anne in the United States alone.

Anne is becoming more sophisticated with age; newer versions of the training doll are ever more advanced. Laerdal Medical works in co-operation with top professionals within emer-

gency medicine, and the firm is held in highest professional esteem around the world.

The founder of this enterprise was Åsmund S. Lærdal, who started out many years ago making plastic dolls and toys. Lærdal died in 1981, but the firm continues in family hands.

Electric power

Lyse Kraft, the electric power company, supplies 75% of Rogaland's population with electricity. 245.000 people live in the Lyse area, which consists of 18 municipalities, from Egersund in the south to Hjelmeland and Kvitsøy in the north.

Lyse Kraft is an inter-municipal power company. 16 municipalities own the firm, whose purpose is to supply the owner municipalities with electric power. The company produces and sells power wholesale. Eleven power companies sell the electricity further to the individual consumer.

Lyse Kraft owns and operates two power stations at Lysebotn. The Lysebotn power station was begun in 1947 and was ready for use in 1964. It delivers 1.200 million kilowatt hours (GWh) per year, which is the equivalent of consumption by 80.000 people.

Tjodan power station is a smaller installation which was built in less than three years, and was ready in 1984. The Tjodan station produces 310 million kilowatt hours. As a part of this project, a road was built up from Lysebotn and across to Sirdal.

In addition to the power from Lysebotn, Lyse Kraft owns 41.1% of the Sira-Kvina works and 18% of Ulla-Førre.

Lyse Kraft employs about 140 people. The head office is at Tronsholmen in the municipality of Sandnes. This is also the location of the centre which manages and oversees twenty transformer stations in the Lyse area. A similar centre at Lysebotn controls the two power stations located there.

The energy supply for North Rogaland is in charge of Haugesund Energiverk and Karmsund Kraftlag. An additional gas power station at Kårstø will make North Rogaland into a major supplier of energy in the years to come.

Norway's largest power station

The red carpet was unrolled for the Kvilldal power station opening on May 3, 1982 by H.M. King Olav. Kvilldal is Norway's largest power station.

The Ulla-Førre installations have cost Statskraft – the state power company – 7,6 billion kroner. In a county accustomed to dealing in billions, perhaps the sum is not impressive. However, the installations which took 12 years to complete have made their mark upon the border areas between Rogaland and East Agder. Huge reservoirs can hold as much as 3.110.000 million tonnes of water. Enough for quite a bit of energy for household and industry.

It took some 1500 workers to build the installations, but once the three stations are in normal operation it will take no more than thirty or forty people from Suldal and Sauda to run it.

The Ulla-Førre development has been beneficial for the economies of the inner Ryfylke, particularly Suldal. After some hectic years peace will soon descend again when construction is over.

Top photograph shows Strovass-dammen at Bykle in East Agder, which

collects water for the Kvilldal power station, seen at lower right.

We are used to huge concrete constructions in the oil industry, but not even the biggest of them measures up to Strovassdammen, the largest reservoir in the Ulla-Førre system.

Photograph: Jostein Granli.

Energy

"Saudafallene" was established in 1933 and in 1922 the Sauda foundry started its operations. 650 people work at the plant today, half the number employed in the '60s. Manganese ore is shipped to Sauda from South and West Africa, Mexico and Brazil. The foundry was formerly foreign owned, today it belongs to the Elkem concern.

Next page: The aluminium works at Karmøy have been in operation since 1967. They have since been expanded and Hydro Aluminium, Karmøy Fabrikker has 1600 employees. Production capacity has reached 220,000 tonnes.

North Sea Workshops

The crisis in the shipping industry meant ever fewer orders for new buildings for the shipyards of Rosenberg and Haugesunds Mekaniske Verksted. Neither lost any time in providing the oil industry with its necessities. Kværner of Egersund built a new workshop, Kværner Brug, lower left, while at Rosenberg in Stavanger and HMV in Haugesund, at right, they outfitted vessels. The three North Sea workshops employ over 2500 people between them. Their tasks have been enormous; Rosenberg has built the decks for three huge production platforms, Statfjord B the first of them.

Photograph: Åkre and Gundersen. Tor Brekke (at right).

For the world market

Kverneland A/S at Øksnevad, with its huge manufacturing facilities for plows, is almost entirely dependent on export sales.

Just as dependent on foreign sales are Trallfa-Robot A/S, who sell their industrial robots to many customers around the world, among them the automobile indusry. The robots from Jæren are used for spray-painting among other jobs.

The development of Kverneland's new factory complex at Øksnevad started in the 1960s and, as can be seen from the photograph, grown considerably since then.

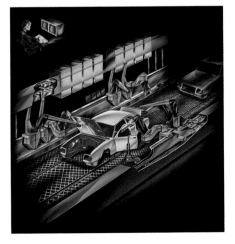

Brøyt A/S at Bryne export 70% of their excavating machines, which cost between 600,000 and 3 million kroner apiece. Turnover in 1987 was 100 million kroner.

Scandinavia's foremost builder of house

Block Watne's is a modern industrial fairy tale. After several generations of a family run lumber business, Gunnar Block Watne started manufacturing and marketing houses in 1955. Since then, Block Watne has become the biggest home manufacturer in Scandinavia. In Norway they build 3000 houses a year at present.

In addition to house building, Block Watne enterprises are also involved in industrial buildings, international marketing and a chain of building supply stores around Norway.

Headquarters of the Block Watne concern is at Øksnevad in Klepp municipality. the organization is decentralised, with 120 offices around the country. The firm consist of Block Watne Homes A/S and Block Watne Marketing A/S.

Following pages: Shopping centres, the huge offices of the oil industry, furniture and appliance emporiums take advantage of lower rents and easy parking at Forus, between Stavanger and Sandnes.

Photo: Olav Garborg.

Norway sold by the piece

Titania A/S at Sokndal is exploiting one of the world's largest titanium sources. Each year six million tonnes of ore and rock are crushed, yielding 885,000 tonnes of ilmenite concentrate. Titania is Norway's third largest mine and employs 350 people.

The plentiful sand in the Ryfylke has been the basis of prosperous undertakings, among them the building of the huge concrete oil platforms. The photograph to the right is from Norsk Sand's quarry at Årdal.

Development

The title of this page could be "good district developers". At top left are the brothers Audun and Kjell Moen, wearing leather fashions made by their firm, Alexander of Moi. Then we see the three Rasmussen brothers, Nils, Leif and Kåre, who have carried on the business started by their Danish father Johs. Rasmussen, since become Scandinavia's largest window factory. Photo: Beckstrøm.

At the edge of the pool sits Jacob Hatteland in Vindafjord, who sells electric components all over Europe. He employs fifty people, whom he provides with nursery school and swimming pool. Photo: Pål Christensen.

The training and com- munications

"Oil drilling" on land at Ullandhaug at the Rogaland research centre. The research centre employs about 150 people – 60% with bachelor's degrees and 37% with doctorates.

Rogalandsdata is now tied in to some 2000 computer terminals. The company employs 233 highly qualified people.

Rogaland County Council owns 60% of the share of Rogalandsdata, who have a major contract with Statoil.

Flags raised in the oil capital

European flags wave in front of the Petroleum Directorate's office complex at Ullandhaug in Stavanger. They have been raised in welcome for the participants of a European gas transporters' conference. Norway is already a significant exporter of gas and will become an even larger one when further fields are developed in years to come. Stavanger became oil capital with the Petroleum Directorate's establishment in town. From a modest beginning, the Directorate now em-

ploys 350 people. Work conditions at their attractive offices are excellent. (See the photograph of the PD on page 236.)

Statoil, the state owned oil company, was also established in Stavanger. A vast office complex has grown up at Forus where Statoil's many sided activities are managed. In 1987 Statoil had 11,000 employees and a turnover of 49 billion kroner.

Phillips Petroleum was the first to discover oil. They operate the Ekofisk field, and other activities on the Norwegian shelf from their offices in Tananger.

Esso, British Petroleum and Amoco also operate their fields from Stavanger, as does Elf Aquitaine Norge A/S, who are in charge of the Frigg and Heimdalfields.

Oil and gas have changed life along the Rogaland coast.

The next few pages show some of the highlights of what began as pure fairy tale and has become a part of daily reality.

The oil county

By: Jan Hagland

Oil county.

We know that, of course. We know all about this oil county, for better or worse. The county of plenty, swimming in milk and honey, and so on. And on.

But there is more to it than that. It is also a gas county for example. Or, a whole gas coast.

Each day, around the clock, Norwegian gas from the Statfjord field is landed at Kalstø on the west of the Ryfylke island of Karmøy, and it is piped further in underground tunnels to Kårstø in Tysvær. There, a sophisticated "dairy" separates the "cream" (butane and ethane) – and sends the skimmed milk (pure natural gas) – through a pipeline to the Ekofisk plant, which in turn takes this Rogaland gas flow to join the mainstream at Emden in West Germany, and further to the Continent.

For the time being, no Norwegian county other than Rogaland can call itself the gas county.

And more is to come: Norway's first gas based thermal power plant will be built at Kårstø, from where a pipeline may eventually cross Boknafjord and supply the gas for another thermal power plant on north Jæren. This increased flow may later be piped further, around to the South Coast and the densely populated eastern part of Norway, on to Sweden and beyond.

Facing the century of gas

These are only plans but they are based on reality, as we are about to enter Norway's century of gas. If the plans are realised, the first developments will take place at Kårstø.

A petrochemical future could also be hovering over the horizon of north Jæren: ammonia, urea or gas for petrol.

Ekofisk field, 1969: the flare burns for the first time on the Ocean Viking, the discoverer of oil on the Norwegian shelf. Next Page: The Ekofisk tank was the first of the concrete giants to be built in Stavanger. *Photograph: Leif Berge.*

Northern Rogaland was picked by the Storting after the first year of oil production, for landing and storing all oil and gas in Norway. At today's production levels we know that there will be gas for the next 120 years. And in time, who knows?

We should perhaps knock on wood; the oil activity has brought the shadows of envy over Rogaland. Rogaland has had enough, they say. Although this is not so, it is a fact that Rogaland's dry land lies next to where the powers of nature – many millions of years ago – arranged for oil and gas to form underneath the compressed geological depths.

Blown by foreign winds

Rogaland is Norway's North Sea county, and Rogalanders have done what former Ocean Reserach Director Gunnar Rollefsen said was a prime condition for any coastal population: they should get to know the sea first, he said. Rogaland's population has certainly learned to use the North Sea as an economic resource; just consider the herring and the shipping eras.

Granted, the oil era blew in on foreign winds. Early in

The jack-up operation became necessary when the seabed sunk unexpectedly by over 4 metres, as a consequence of oil being pumped out from under the surface. It took millimetre precision to raise the platforms by 6 metres, to allow clearance for the "hundred year wave". The operation was successfully accomplished in the summer of 1987.
Photograph: Phillips Petroleum/Husmo Foto.

This was the first jack-up operation of the kind ever conducted. The Ekofisk accomodation platform was the first to be lifted. The picture on the following page shows activity on the field in the summer of 1987.
Photograph: Phillips Petroleum/Husmo Foto.

the '60s the international oil industry saw their task: if they were to maintain their position as the world's most important energy supplier, they must then move off the land and into the sea.

The North Sea came into focus through the huge gas discovery made in 1959 under the grain fields of the Dutch province of Groningen. Geologists drew the conclusion that it must be the same geological structure extending into the North Sea. However, there was a border at Jutland in Denmark and towards British territory, because according to theories of the time, this ancient deposit of sedimentation must have come from the south.

Still valid on the Norwegian shelf?

Meanwhile, geologists with an oil company named Phillips Petroleum Company Co. in Bartlesville, Oklahoma – deep inland in the United States – figured that the same geological sedimentary accumulations could also have come from the north. That is, that the Norwegian Shelf could be attractive after all. Norway has honoured one of these geologists, Ward Dunn, with the nation's highest distinction, the St. Olav award.

Thus, Phillips came to Norway and applied for sole licence of the Norwegian shelf. In return, Norway was to get a seismic programme worth a million dollars – the equivalent of a good 7 million kroner. Seven million in exchange for the Norwegian shelf. Norway asked Phillips for time to consider; we had no precedents to cover a situation such as this one.

32 dry holes

The American drill ship Ocean Traveller spudded its first well on the Norwegian shelf on July 1, 1966, under licence 001. Several summers and 32 dry holes were to pass before the Ekofisk field was discovered on December 23, 1969.

Norway became overnight a member of a very exclusive club of oil producing countries in the world. With the discovery of Ekofisk, the state realised that it must become involved economically and strategically.

Norway's consumption for 400 years

After over 20 years of oil and gas exploration, we have a proven deposit of 5 billion tonnes of oil equivalents in the North Sea, enough for Norway's use for 400 years. Only ten percent of this has been produced so far.

The Norwegian Petroleum Directorate – which had since moved to Stavanger – announced in mid-1987 that there

Previous page: Tow-out of the Beryl platform to the British sector. Elf Aquitaine is operator of the Frigg and Heimdal gas fields.
Below: Elf's headquarters at Dusavika in Stavanger.
At right: View of the Frigg field.
Next Page: Like a gigantic honeycomb, the Gullfaks C platform taking shape at Norwegian Contractors' site at Hinnavågen.
* Photograph: Leif Berge.*

Storm on the Statfjord field. From an oil worker's daily life.   *Photograph: Leif Berge*

could well be another 5 billion tonnes to be found under the Norwegian Shelf. Naturally it is hoped that there is even more, although accepting that there could be less; in this industry it is only drilling that tells. In either case, we have ahead of us exploration plans reaching to the year 2020.

Waiting for Askeladden

By that time the oil county will have reached the peak of life, but we know that regardless of oil jobs, the gas coast will still be alive. Besides, it is on average only 30 percent of the available oil which is extracted under its own pressure; with a bit of help it should be possible to extract more. Technological reserach is hard at work on this; the North Sea area is just waiting for the fairy tale ingenuity of Askeladden.

The oil industry is moving northward. New bases are being built around Harstad and Hammerfest while the

(Cont'd. pg. 140)

A giant of a crane

Rogalanders have become accustomed to larger than life scales. Nowadays, a giant like this hardly merits a second glance. The pictures were taken at the time Statfjord B was assembled at Rosenberg shipyard in Stavanger. Balder, the 3000 tonne capacity mammoth, did the heavy work.

Photograph: Leif Berge.

The price we pay. Producing oil has its price, paid for in human lives. The greatest tragedy occured when the Alexander Kielland platform capsized on March 27, 1980. One hundred and twenty three people died. A monument to keep their memory alive was erected at Kvernevik in Stavanger. It is the work of sculptor Johannes Block Hellum, who won a competition with his design.

Photograph: Agnes Sævig.

northern part of the North Sea, including Statfjord, Gullfaks and Oseberg, is operated from Bergen.

Still, the headquarters remain in Stavanger. Headquarters as long as there is anything to harvest from the Norwegian Shelf, however long that may last.

Vacuuming the North Sea

It is probable that the Ekofisk area will continue to be viable until the year 2040, possibly until 2060. Norsk Hydro has just recently made a promising discovery in block 9/2 near the Danish border; Statoil has found oil in the so-called Egersund basin just off Egersund. We are getting ready for the 12th round of concessions in 1988, when the North Sea is to be vacuumed. It is said that a 13th and a 14th round are to follow.

Here and there are many smaller and larger oil pools at which no production attempts have been made so far. New technology allows the industry to look again at formerly proven good areas. Neither seismic tehnology nor geological theory stand still; ever new tools are found, new ways of approaching problems.

Reaching into the next century

Local administrative organizations will be found elsewhere, whether the companies agree or not. The oil industry is still used as an element in district development in Norway, although the Storting has realised that the situation demands more sober thinking.

For Stavanger, or North Jæren, the vital decision continues: the headquarters remain here. This is a policy laid down ever since the start for oil exploration in

The oil industry must at all times be prepared to meet accidents. The photograph on the right shows a fire drill at the safety training school in Haugesund.
Photograph: Tor Brekke.

Norway. This will mean that unless Norwegian oil policy is totally changed, the entire international oil industry will continue with us until the next century. The book "Norge og verden" ("Norway and the world") says that Stavanger is Europe's most international city – judged by education and income – as if it was something to feel apologetic about; it says that one of the world's most advanced industries is operated from Stavanger. Economically the most dynamic industry in the world, surpassed only by the weapons industry.

Most vital marginal producer

Although Norway is not one of the major producers of oil in the world, we are in any case – in the eyes of OPEC – the world's most important marginal producer because we export 90 percent of the total production.

In the course of a few short years Statoil will be selling more oil and gas to the world market from their sales offices in Stavanger than Shell and Conoco. The significance of this is that in Norway, in Stavanger at Forus if you like, sits a newly established Norwegian company which deals in one of the world's most important strategical commodities, on par with the biggest in the world.

Nothing but the best

And what does that tell us? That in Stavanger there is the ability – in a number of enterprises – to deal with with economy, technology and industry on the highest level. Because of the oil industry's significance in human terms and regarding security; for the economy and the environment, it means that all activity must be served by an expertise on a level that accepts nothing but the best.

What consequences this sort of capacity – whether educated at home or at universities and colleges abroad – will bring to a city and county living at close quarters with the oil industry for 21 years is anybody's guess.

West Vision

To the right we see the West Vision. It took almost two months for this rig to make its way, self-propelled, from Korea to Stavanger through the Suez Canal. The West Vision was built for Smedvig Drilling and sold to Statoil for 800 million kroner. It will become one of the permanent instal-

lations on the Veslefrikk field. Among Stavanger shipping companies, Smedvig has best coped with the transition from shipping to oil in a decade of crisis in the shipping industry.

Smedvig employs 750 people.

They have been awarded long term contracts by Statoil and they also drill in the British sector through a daughter company, Dan-Smedvig.

Photograph: Sigurd Tang-Wa.

New life in an old building

Mobil Exploration Norway employed tact and a fine sense of esthetics in restoring old canneries along Strandkaien to serve as their offices.

Mobil has been the operator of the Statfjord field until 1987 and has several concessions in a number of other blocks on the Norwegian shelf. The sailing ship is the Christian Radich.

A "troll" tamed

The picture to the right shows the production platform on the Troll field superimposed on Stavanger harbour, dwarfing the city. A huge project; when totally developed it will have cost 24 billion Norwegian kroner (at 1987 value). Troll is the largest offshore gas field in existence, from top to the platform measures 460 metres – almost half a kilometre.

Operator of the project is A/S Norske Shell.

Oil show

The Siddis Centre – Stavanger's modern exhibition and conference complex – has become, in the space of a few years, one of Norway's leading fair and congress venues. A prime reason for this has been the biennial international oil show, the Offshore Northern Seas Conference and Exhibition, ONS for short.

From a humble start in 1974 with 200 exhibitors ONS has grown into the leading international forum for the offshore industry. 750 companies rented stands at the 1986 event. Visitors also multiplied; from 9000 in 1974 to about 30,000 by 1986.

ONS openings have regularly been honoured by a royal representative. H.M. King Olav (bottom of page) here, being shown around the exhibition area by ONS Executive Chairman Finn Lied, and Stavanger Forum's Director, Per Olav Hanssen.

The addition of a new Conference Centre for Stavanger Forum (lower left) in 1982 has brought the entire complex to international standards. Stavanger has become a leading fair and congress town because of the up to date facilities of the Siddis Centre.

Gro lights the flame

Prime Minister Gro Harlem Brundtland was given the honour of setting alight the gas flame which symbolised the opening of the Kårstø terminal on August 25, 1986. This is the main junction of Statpipe, the pipe network that carries gas to the Norwegian coast.

Statpipe has been built in order to supply gas to European industry. Next to the Prime Minister stands Statoil's former Administrative Director, Arve Johnsen.

On this page, top: the Kårstø installation. It cost 2 billion kroner less to build than originally estimated.

Bottom: a huge pipe-laying barge, curving past Karmøy.

Photograph: Statoil.

Communication

By: Lars Chr. Sande

When the priest Alexander Lange, grandfather of Alexander Kielland on his mother's side, moved to Stavanger from Asker in 1818, he and his entourage had a rather heavy journey. First across the winter snow and ice with horse and sled to Christiansand, and from there by sailing vessel. They used all of three weeks on the stretch of sea to Egersund, and then came to an abrupt stop at Hellvik, since winter storms made it impossible to cross the Jæren sea. The travelling party were able to hire some horses from a farm and so they rode on towards Stavanger, which at that time was described as further away and more isolated than even Finnmark.

When the Southland railway line was opened in 1944 it seemed a dream come true, although it was soon over shadowed by the German occupation during World War II. However, the journey between Stavanger and Oslo could now be done in ten hours, on one train.

Today, it takes a half hour to fly between Fornebu in Oslo, and Stavanger Airport at Sola.

Talk about progress.

The queasy coastal route

Before the Southland railway was inaugurated, the main form of transportation between Stavanger and Oslo were coastal liners. A particular nightmare for many was the stretch along the Jæren coast and around Lista, where it helped not at all that the ships were stately vessels or that the captains were firm and competent.

Although Haugesund now has an airport at Karmøy with daily service to Fornebu as well as regular flights to Bergen and Stavanger, the rest of the fjord and island filled county of Rogaland still depends on ships and ferries, and will continue to do so for some time to come. Modern car ferries have been put into service and it is now possible to take one's car to the remotest of islands, such as Utsira.

New trains have been put into service on the southland railway line. More powerful engines make for faster speed, and the new carriages for comfortable travel. In spite of this, airplanes still win hands down in the competitition for passengers between Stavanger and Oslo.

Photograph: Jan Ingemundsen.

On the following page we see the Concorde about to land at Sola airport. The new terminal building keeps receiving travellers' approval.

Photograph: Egil Eriksson.

Express boat revolution

The boat designer Ludvig Thorsen of Det Stavanger Dampskibsselskap – the Stavanger steamship company – put the finishing touch on his design for what he called the new "fjord bus" in the late 1930s. Not only were these new express boats more comfortable, but they were considerably faster than the old fjord steamers. Travel time was cut down yet again.

Hydrofoils arrived in the 1960s, crossing the waves at automobile speed. They served, among others, Stavanger and Bergen. Today it is the Westamaran which is used for the express route, and even newer, faster boats are expected.

The most modern airport in Norway

When it was built in 1937, Stavanger Airport at Sola was the country's first civil airport. The 50th anniversary of this event was celebrated in 1987, with a two day air show. The new terminal building was just finished in time for the event and with its completion, Sola Airport can justifiedly boast being the most modern in Norway.

The Stavanger Airport was intended for more international traffic than it has had. However, it is an important traffic junction.

The main workshop of the domestic airline Braathen is located at Sola.

Helikopter Service operates their fleet of helicopters that serve North Sea oil installations from Forus.

Modern bus fleet

Bus travel from Rogaland to destinations in Europe has been popular ever since before the war. By now the local fleet of buses has grown, carrying tourists to tempting places in Scandinavia and beyond. The fleet consists of the latest and most modern in bus design, both single and double deckers.

Express boats

The old steamers took their time along the Rogaland coast until 1939, when Det Stavangerske Dampskibsselskap – the Stavanger Steam Ship Company – placed the fjord bus "Fjordrott" into sevice. She was a new design, built by Ludvig Thorsen. Several new versions of this speedy newcomer followed. DSD was a pioneer in the field and did not rest on their laurels. A fleet of hydrofoils were added to the coastal route in the 1960s. Since then, through joining forces with Flaggruten, Westamarans have joined the Stavanger–Bergen route.

The boat in the picture is "Karmsund", which was taken over by DSD when it bought out HSD, the steam ship company of Haugesund.

Photograph: Tor Brekke.

Next page: Ferry quay at Skudeneshavn, on the day without a long queue.

Photograph: Tor Brekke.

Although most freight nowadays is carried on land, coastal traffic is still important. The pictures on these pages reflect a seaman's lot on coastal routes. Life was a good deal more dangerous in the days before accurate sea charts, markers and lighthouses showed the way.

Norges Sjøkartverk – the Norwegian navigation chart makers – have their headquarters in Stavanger, from where they keep track of all that takes place at sea.
Photograph: Tor Brekke. Left: Inge Bruland.

Newspapers and local radio

Haugesund has a daily newspaper, Haugesunds Avis, while Stavanger has three dailies: Rogalands Avis, Stavanger Aftenblad and Rogaland.

The Stavanger Aftenblad, thanks to profitable management, has built up a modern newspaper business with 300 employees, about 90 of them editorial staff. Stavanger's press has long enjoyed a fine reputation.

The emergence of local radio has brought new challenges. A number of stations are operated by different groups and local communities in Rogaland. Stavanger has Radio Vest and Siddis Radio, the former possibly one of the most professional of the local radio operations in the country. Eigersund has Okka Radio and Dalane TV.

In touch with the world around us

Stavanger's position as the oil capital of Norway has lead to a speedy development of telecommunication services. What was once an isolated corner of Norway is now in contact with the rest of the world, as befitting a most modern society.

Communication is, however, to be improved further. A ferry-less coastal road to Kristiansund is the great goal. In addition, ferry connections are planned for Rennesøy and the Ryfylke across Høgsfjorden. Some of the plans are so advanced that, considering the speed of developments, a ferry-less crossing of the Westland fjords can become a reality not long beyond the turn of the millenium.

Air travel centre

The headquarters of Braathens Safe are at Sola, where they employ 630 people in airplane maintenance, serving thirty airlines.

Helikopter Service is another major concern. Without helicopters it would be almost impossible to conduct offshore oil exploration and production with any degree of efficiency. Helikopterservice employs 700 people. Their turnover in 1986 was 800 million kroner.

Ocean of people at Sola Festival

Over 30.000 visitors came to see the celebration of Stavanger Airport's 50th anniversary on May 29-30, 1987. Although fewer than expected by the organizers, the crowd was still the largest that had ever been attracted to any event held in Rogaland. The viewers were treated to show airplanes and stunts from morning till late in the afternoon, one spectacular feat after the other.

It was the famed "Red Arrows" of the British Royal Air Force who got the most ahhhhs. These nine flying aces, recognised world champions, put their red Hawk Hunters through routines in precision formation flying that seemed to defy the laws of God,man and machine. As when two of the Arrows flew towards each other at top speed, appearing certain to crash just a few feet above the runway – only to both tip sideways at the very last instant, flying past each other practically belly to belly. (See following pages.)

90 events were packed into the programme. Never before has such a vast air show been held in this country. 130 planes from eight different nations took part and 70 exhibition planes came from countries all over Europe.

Among these was the first plane that ever landed at Sola, on May 6, 1937: a Junker Ju-52 passenger plane belonging to *Det Norske Luftfartsselskap* in those days. She returned to Sola wearing Lufthansa's colours, sweeping across Jæren and Hafrsfjord as majestically as she did she inaugerated the airport.

Tourism

By: Pelle Nilssen

The Rogalander, with his focus aimed at the world, has always been prone to wanderlust. He is well located, he has most of what makes Norway such an exceptional tourist attraction right at home and, in addition, he is a close neighbor to the rest of Europe.

Immigrants and visitors see the qualities of Rogaland possibly more clearly than most natives. Should we be a bit prouder of where we are, of where our home is?

Should we open our eyes to the treasures around us? The tantalizing, bedazzling versatility of the landscape, the cultural history and the different life styles that the county embraces? It is a land of tension between the harsh west coast and the mild south coast, in both physical and emotional senses.

From a virtual standstill, tourism in Rogaland has taken off with gusto in the last few years. Ideas and visions -both lofty and down to earth -have been allowed to grow in full freedom.

There are times when summer and skiing co-exist, resulting in attire like this.   *Photograph: Tor Brekke*

Much more than holidays and July

Tourism is so infinitely more than holidays and July. Tradionally tourism has meant recreation travel. Unexpectedly, mass tourism in Norway actually started in Rogaland; the first foreign charter tour to Norway came in 1885 with an English group who were to take the "Discovery Route". These trendsetters travelled from Stavanger to Sand, up Suldal to Nesflaten and through Bratlandsdalen to Føldal, from where they would continue further to Hardanger and Voss.

Small fjord-side hotels, simple boarding houses, private lodgings, modest tourist huts and eventually, tents and a few cruise ships; this is what tourism in Rogaland consisted of for many years. And foreigners who sought the exotic, along with energetic locals equipped with backpacks, enthusiasm and heavy skis. Tourism meant also Easter and fjord boats, not forgetting Mr. Archer who saw the potential of Suldal far back in 1885. He gathered up all the salmon rights, brought his friends and acquaintances over, and the "salmon lords" conquered Suldal. It granted the area a measure of fame that it still rides upon.

The popular fjords

The Ryfylke fjord area has always been the most popular place for excursions for both visitors and for the people of Stavanger and Sandnes, while the Haugeland fjords were most enjoyed by people from Haugesund. The upper classes occupied choice green spots for their country places and gradually more and more cottages were built, bringing variable relations between townsman and peasant.

Steamships and the romance associated with quaysides disappeared once ferries, cars and rapid boats became a daily affair, which contributed to changing the old fjord atmosphere . Conditions changed and traditional tourism in Rogaland was neglected. Jobs disappeared and few new ones were created, especially for women.

"Tourist" an insult

Some of the localities were accustomed to tourists and took them as a source of income and stimulation. However, there was many a place were "tourist" was a dirty word, where it represented an instrusion and disturbance, where it upset the values and the local traditions. There are still corners of Rogaland where this attitude persists.

Aside from a lack of pride and faith in the value of what we can offer, communication barriers are the greatest obstacle for the development of tourism in many localities. Furthermore, neither accommodation nor choice of activities are sufficient.

A jewel on the West Coast

Skudeneshavn on Karmøy island is a popular excursion place. Foreign tourists in particular delight in this small town full of carefully preserved old houses. Skudeneshavn is the largest Norwegian town where so much is left unchanged from the last century.

Conservation started with a group of people in the '50s, unusual in those days when most of coastal Norway was intent on pulling down the old wooden houses and replacing them with concrete blocks.

A stroll through the mellow streets of Skudeneshavn can act as an antidote to the stress of fast paced modern life.

Below: Also Haugesund has small wooden houses.

Photograph: Tor Brekke.

Konge-
parken

Over 220.000 people visited the amusement park Kongeparken at Gjesdal during its first season in 1986, before it was
forced to declare bankruptcy. Spareban-
ken Rogaland took over as the largest
mortgagee and by the next season, in
1987, there was life and activity once
more in the park, plus a number of new
attractions.   Photograph: Roy Storvik.

If fell to eight year old Ann Michell Jørpeland, along with SAS boss Janne Carlzon, to cut the red ribbon and mark the opening of the SAS Royal Hotel in Stavanger. The pictures to the left show the interior of the hotel and the Løkkeveien façade. On the facing page we see the KNA Hotel, which has been considerably expanded and redecorated in recent years. Stavanger's hotel capacity has been enlarged during a one year hotel boom by about 60%.

Mostly for the best

The discovery of oil has been influential for the hotel industry of Rogaland, particularly of Stavanger; beneficial for the most part, but not entirely. The holidaying traveller has become less financially rewarding for hotels than businessmen. When prices shot up recreational travel almost disappeared.

At the same time, Stavanger gained a reputation for fully booked hotels, a difficult situation for a city hoping to attract ever more visitors.

Gradually, new hotels were built and existing ones expanded until North Jæren and Haugesund stood ready with an almost 70% increase in hotel capacity in the course of one year. This happened at about the same time that the price of oil fell drastically and, along with it, the activity level of the Norwegian oil industry. Hoteliers' concerns turned to over-supply and unoccupied beds. The result has been intensive marketing, and hope for the future.

Liquor licensing laws have been a bone of contention, often tied to the tourist industry. A revolutionary change in outlook took place, beginning in Haugesund and spreading to the towns in the south of the county. The present result has been 70 establishments licensed to serve alcohol in Stavanger alone. There are more people going out at night, and staying out later, than ever before.

Breiavatnet, the very heart of Stavanger. The building to the right of the Atlantic Hotel is the head office of Rogalandsbanken.

Before and after the Atlantic Hotel

Touristic time in Stavanger is reckoned as pre- and post-Atlantic Hotel. When the hotel was opened in 1952, it was as if a breeze had blown in from the wide open world. The hotel has grown since that time, most of the interior has been renovated and many times redecorated. Newer and more elegant restaurants opened such as the Antique,

in 1987. However, in spite of the renovations, one restaurant has remained a fixture all these years: Mortepumpen. Originally it was designed by the City Antiquarian, architect Einar Hedén, the man whose name has become synonymous with the preservation of Stavanger's architectural heritage. The Mortepumpen restaurant, with its faça-

des of old houses along "Stranden" quay in Stavanger – Straen, as it is affectionately called locally – wraps diners in characteristic Stavanger atmosphere.

The Atlantic Hall was built in the '60s, the largest concert hall in town in those days. The hall is still often in use,

especially for large meetings and conferences.

The professionalism of the Atlantic Hotel has come to mean much for the town's business in general. Few Norwegian cities are able to offer so much hotel accommodation and so many eating places in fact, as Stavanger can.

A rare fine day at Godalen in Stavanger with the tall ship Statsråd Lemkuhl on the fjord. Photo: Lars Chr. Sande. Picture opposite shows Sola Strand Hotel which has its charm even in the winter. Below left: The large diningroom with its floor planks from an old Norwegian naval vessel. Another hotel dining room is decorated with artefacts from an old passenger ship, the Mount Royal.

Norwegian cuisine

Norwegians have begun to realise that their cooking is something to be proud of. A new generation of Norwegian chefs are combining the best of French and Norwegian cooking skills and reaping praises at home and abroad for their efforts. This is particularly noticeable in Rogaland, where the enjoyment of good food is gaining ground. In fact, Stavanger is increasingly referred to as the gourmet's place to eat.

In order to further develop a hospitable environment, it is necessary to reinforce both training and the concept of service throught education. The Rogaland county administration, in its concern for the growth of tourism, is making an effort to strengthen travel education in local colleges.

The Norwegian hotel training school has been in operation in Rogaland since 1952, first at the Sola Strand Hotel, then in their own building at Ullandhaug. It has recently been accredited as a college and is about to be recognised all over Scandinavia. The majority of Norwegian hotel administrators have received their professional training in Rogaland, and the impression is that they are satisfied with the results.

And then came Kongeparken

What we all wanted was the cherry on the top. A special attraction for the family, for children. We got Kongeparken and with that addition Rogaland has raised its standing among Norwegian tourist spots by several notches.

The idea originated with local tourist authorities, but after that it was the landowner's show. Gabriel Ålgård flew into action and created something new: for Gjesdal, for Rogaland and for Norway. A park took shape faster than one could imagine. Vast and lovely and expensive. So expensive that bankruptcy was inevitable not long after opening in the summer of 1986. The SR-Bank, which had financed the park, stepped in and took over.

An effective, high level marketing campaign attracted 220.000 visitors to Kongeparken during the first season. Rogalanders tended to wait and see, but the rest of the country came. The summer of 1987 evened this out somewhat, but the future of this grandly planned amusement park remains uncertain.

The tallest pulpit in the world

The vestments of two priests flutter in the wind. The congregation sits on rocks and on tufts of grass and, way below them, gleams the Lysefjord. Five trumpeters from the Forsand school band carry the tune of a hymn, and Bjørn Bue, Bishop of Stavanger (on the left), and Pastor Bjørn Brakstad stand with their feet firmly planted on the mightiest pulpit in the world, "Prekestolen".

These were the words the Stavanger Aftenblad used to describe a religious service somewhat out of the ordinary. It took place one Sunday in June of 1987.

It was the Bishop himself who, as part of an official visit to the Høgsfjord parish, hit upon the idea that a Mass this Sunday atop Prekestolen would be a fine idea. And, where else in the world is there room on the pulpit for both priests and congregation?

Photograph: Finn Refvem.

If you are lucky the fish will bite

We don't dare to promise that everyone who tries his luck fishing will be as well rewarded as this young man. The currents are influenced by wind and weather and in northwesterlies the fish simply will not bite. But then, to compensate, come evenings when the line goes taut with regularity and the thrill is whether you will be able to land them all?

Should you manage one like this, there is nothing in the world like freshly caught cod, unless it is salmon which still gleams here and there in Rogaland's rivers. Salmon have even been known to take the bait under water – but that is practically like hitting the jackpot.

Photograph: Tor Brekke.

Pleasant shopping

Increased buying power tends to find an outlet in increased spending. Thus, large shopping centres have appeared in several places around Rogaland, bringing about changed shopping habits – often to the detriment of the local corner shop. Ease of parking has become the great come-on for shoppers, and one of the main reasons for the success of suburban shopping complexes. In spite of new parking halls built in Stavanger, it can take a while to find a place to leave a car at the busier times. However, businesses have taken up the challenge and several major projects have seen the light of day in recent years, while others are under construction.

One of the most successful of these is Lærdal Eiendom's *Breitorget,* a whole city block of old Stavanger houses in the heart of the city, that have been renovated and joined internally in a series of galleries on different levels, with a glass-roofed courtyard in the centre. The courtyard serves as a type of village square with an undercover "outdoor" café, surely the ideal solution to Stavanger's weather. The result is a delightful example of how the old can be enjoyed in new ways. As soon as it was opened, Breitorget became a part of the Stavanger downtown scene, always full of life, and therefore attracting more life. Breitorget has been awarded an international prize for exemplary shopping centres.

To the left we see the courtyard of the complex. Breitorget has 17 different businesses, including two restaurants. Above, to the right, are old houses, some as much as 160 years old, setting the seal of continuity on today's city life.

In Haugesund, Haraldsgate is the place to shop, particularly on a sunny Saturday morning.

Photograph: Tor Brekke.

Havens of pleasure

Arild and Kjetil Friestad meet the very founder of the park at Nærbø, Randulf Aadnesen, 93. Aadnesen dug this garden out of a peat bog on his property. A great variety of birds live in the park, thanks to Aadnesen, brother of shopkeeker Eme- lankton A. who is mentioned on page 240. Photograph: Jonas Friestad.

At Tau we find another haven, by the old mills. They started their existence in the service of the Tou A/S mill and bre- wery, who also own Christiansand Brewery. The firm had a turnover of 441 million kroner in 1986. A brand new brewery has been erected at Forus in Stavanger, employing 250 people.

ROGALAND sets the table

Text: Borhild Fiskå
Photographs: Jonas Friestad

Rogaland sets tables nowadays all over the world. The dinnerware on Kloster's luxury liners is made at Figgjo. The Høyang-Polaris saucepans and casseroles which Ingrid Espelid has been using for years on her TV cooking show is often to be seen in the pages of Danish and Swedish cooking magazines.

The popular daily, Verdens Gang, has claimed that Stavanger has become the country's top restaurant town. Sandnes-born chef of *Jan's Mat og Vinhus* in Stavanger, Harald Osa, was hailed as the Chef of the Year by his colleagues. We hold our position as top tomato growers. And, furthermore, the legendary chef of King Olav, Tora Skjæveland, is by no means alone in claiming that Rogaland lamb is unmatched in quality anywhere in the world.

Hens lay more eggs in Rogaland than in any other county. On Jæren you will find a dairy research centre, proving that Rogaland is ahead on the milk front as well. Jarlsberg cheese, from Nærbø and from other quality

Top quality foodstuffs served in style, all "made in Rogaland".

dairies around the county, is as much in demand in the United States, Japan and Australia as it is domestically.

Yes, we manage. Our Lord has placed us in a fertile corner of the country. He has also equipped us with enterprising businessmen and with persistent farmers. In the seas He placed a multitude of fish. When the catch became too scarce to provide a livelihood, fish farming was started as a new way of life, creating new jobs and plenty of good fish for all.

Which was the herring town in the old days? Haugesund. Haugesunders will not let us forget that. What about the canning town which supplied Nor-

way and the world with brisling sardnes? That was Stavanger. Foreign influence has been streaming in throughout the years. And, for all we know, it may have been necessary for outsiders to discover how much we have that is good in our southwestern corner of the country, before we ourselves became aware of our riches.

We must admit we owe a modest thanks to our neighboring counties the south: Rogaland lamb is best, we don't relent on that, but it is true that a good part of the flock have grazed themselves tasty on the mountain herbs of Agder county. Still, it is Rogaland this time. And bon appétit!

Rogalamb

Lamb is a meat that Rogalanders have always been on good terms with. Our ancestors have prepared lamb or mutton in all variations and in all their parts. The head was saved for broth to cook dumplings in, the local delicacy called *komler*. In some parts of the country a banquet of *smalaføde* – mutton trotters – is still considered one of the culinary highlights of the year.

Lamb has been salted, dried and smoked. Before the ubiquitous deep freezer, brine barrels of lamb stood in every cellar, providing meat throughout the year.

Pinnekjøtt, pieces of mutton cooked slowly over juniper branches, is a popular west coast dish.

Photographs: Top: Roast lamb with scalloped potatoes is fine Rogaland party food. Left: Chef of the Year 1986, Harald Osa, with a festively dressed leg of lamb. Next page: Dried leg of mutton in the open air, outside the old rectory at Hå.

Cheese county

The elite among Norwegian cheeses is Jarlsberg. Great ten kilo cheeses with the Jarslberg emblem on them travel all over the world from the country's largest cheese deposit at Klepp.

A continuingly popular milk product is *gomme,* or *dravle* as it is called in some places. This traditional food, which was given its own particular taste according to each cook, was made in Rogaland with whole milk, sugar and thickening.

Top: The pride of Norwegian cheese production – Jarlsberg. Next page: Signe Randa at Judaberg serves Ryfylke gomme.

Delicacies of the sea

Rogalanders have much to thank the sea for. Throughout history it has satisfied wanderlust, provided fresh impulses and a livelihood for many. The Rogaland fisherman – whether he is a man alone in his wooden boat or part of a large scale industry on distant seas – has the reputation of a thorough professional.

Fish satisfied many in the days when families were large and incomes small. Fish today is once more sought after because it is nutritious and because it tastes good. Ask any cook and you will be told that fish is the greatest challenge of all because the possiblilities are so many.

Many visitors to Rogaland recall with pleasure days spent browsing throught market and harbourside, examining the fishermen's crates of live crabs ready for boiling. Picking them can be the summer's most risk-filled enterprise: full of tasty meat, or a dud?

Formerly disdained fish have now become popular and fish-farmers are managing to breed new types of fish not available before. And, for those who do not harvest their own, mussel and oyster farms make shellfish accessible. There is no doubt that Rogalanders and fish are a team.

Photograph on opposite page: Master chefs of Rogaland compete yearly for the best meal from the sea at their Neptune Evening, here presented by Lauritz W. Hansen.

Below: The salmon rose that was part of the menu which won Harald Osa the "Golden Chef's Hat".

"Takk for maten" to our ancestors

In the days when knowledge about nutrition and about sensible use of the scarce foodstuffs was rudimentary, a handful of idealists launched themselves into enlightening the public. One of these women was Hulda Garborg, married to the writer Arne Garborg and thus a Rogalander by marriage, although she refers to herself in her writing as the "Kolbotn woman".

Hulda Garborg published books which, in addition to recipes and cooking methods, also gave good advice. "Housekeeping for small households, preferably in the country" was the title of one of them.

Good advice about housekeeping is also dispensed by the pen of Dorthea Rabbe who made her contribution by collecting and publishing local recipes. Rabbe was also the first director of the *Sømme husmorskole* – a domestic sciences school - at Sola from 1917.

The unostentatious recipes published by the two women have stood in sharp contrast to "Den Kiellandske Kokebok" which tends to portray a cooking style overflowing with plenty, influenced by foreign tastes which only a bare minimum of Rogalanders had the chance to enjoy.

Photographs:
Top left: Knudaheio: the way the country cottage of Arne and Hulda Garborg looks today.

Below: Hulda Garborg's portrait behind a decorated table with Munkur — a type of doughnut without the hole — made from a recipe in her own cookbook.

Pears in mountain cranberry sauce. "Downright good and cheap," wrote Hulda Garborg. Here seen with Jarnbrød.

Market stall owners Erna Olsen and Reidar Grodem from Tasta.

Rogaland — kitchen garden

If we include all the greenhouses, we can safely say that Rogaland is the country's earliest producer. Along with spring come the cucumbers and tomatoes and the early potatoes from Randaberg, long before the last snowdrifts have given up in other parts of the country.

As we learned in geography at school, the Ryfylke islands are blessed with unusually good soil. We also have some very entrprising greenhouse farmers who have placed Rennesøy and Finnøy islands at the top of tomato production; 17 of every 18 Norwegian tomatoes are grown in Rogaland.

Whatever produce it is possible to grow in Norway, grows in plentiful supply in Rogaland. Root vegetables have become fashionable once more.

Photographs on next page: Top: Strawberries and cream are nice, but festive strawberries can be prepared the way Chef Knut Juvkam does them.

Below: Stuffed tomatoes, a simple delicacy.

Right: Bengal chutney; a tasty tomato dish.

Poultry county

One of every four eggs that is laid, sold and eaten in Norway is produced by a Rogaland hen. The Rogaland egg co-operative in Sandnes delivers 11 million kilos of eggs a year, according to 1986 figures. Only one fifth of these do we manage to eat ourselves, so Rogaland producers supply the rest of the country with eggs.

Many eggs mean many hens. This is obvious from the statistics of poultry butchering, carried out by the egg co-operative for its 850 members in the entire county, as well as for the co-operative in West Agder county. Altogether 1389 tons of poultry were butchered in 1986, consisting mostly of hens and chickens.

Opposite page: The great strawberry cake, (see recipe above) for a garden party. Right: Turkey has become a popular party dish.

The great strawberry ice cream cake

Base:
4 egg whites
100 gr. icing sugar
200 gr. almonds
Strawberry ice cream:
4 eggs yolks
4 tablespoons sugar
1 dl. strawberry jam
(or mashed fresh strawberries)
5 dl. whipping cream
1/2 dl. brandy
350 gr. marzipan (ready made)
500 gr. fresh strawberries

Whip egg whites stiffly and stir in the icing sugar mixed with the ground almonds. Pur this into a buttered 24 cm. cake pan and bake at 150 C degrees for about 35 minutes. Cool in the pan and make the ice cream.

Beat egg yolks and sugar until white. Fold in carefully jam, whipped cream and brandy. Pour over the cold almond base. Allow the cake to stiffen in the freezer. Cut out a 20 cm. diametre circle in wax paper and lay it on top of the frozen ice cream. Place the cake on a tray, roll out marzipan betweeen two plastic sheets to form a circle large enough to cover the whole cake. Lift the marzipan with the help of one of the plastic sheets and lay it over the cake. Cut a number of small crosses in the marzipan and fold the corners of the crosses back so you get an attractive opening in the centre of the cake. Pull out the wax paper through this opening. The cake can now successfully be frozen.

Blue Bell Crockery: simple and stylish.

Every day beauty from Figgjo

Figgjo A.S. in Sandnes has made a point of brightening the weekday table. They do this whether we sit down to the breakfast table at home, set with "Blue Bell" crockery, or if we wake to a morning of luxury cruising on board the S/S Norway in the Caribbean.

Most people meet Figgjo crockery in restaurants, hotel dining rooms and in institutions. The main market is Scandinavia, with Norway herself using 60% of the production. Of Figgjo's export, 40% goes mainly to the rest of Scandinavia, Switzerland, The United States, and to the Norwegian cruise fleet.

Figgjo's quality products of modern design cover all needs within public catering.

In order to emphasize the lasting quality of their products, Figgjo gives a one year guarantee on merchandise sold to the private consumer. Public consumers are given an "edge guarantee", promising replacement of any item that is chipped.

Stainless bestseller

Høyang-Polaris takes part in food preparation in most Norwegian kitchens. Nowadays the old coffee pot has been replaced by a percolator in most homes, but if one is still in use, more than likely it was made by Høyang-Polaris.

Much of the Norwegian market is covered by Høyang-Polaris. In addition to pots and pans in stainless steel, they also make kitchen utensils in copper, cast iron and aluminium.

The home market is the most significant for Høyang-Polaris as well. Scandinavia is the major export customer.

In Sweden they colaborate with Skultuna and in Denmark with Kløverblad.

Great Britain and the United States are also important customers of kitchen utensils and 8% of Britishers choose Høyang-Polaris when they buy stainless steel saucepans.

Attractive simplicity and pleasurable use: kitchen utensils from Høyang-Polaris.

Rogaland dumplings with suet

10 large peeled potatoes, raw
2 boiled potatoes
1 cup oatmeal
salt
approx. 3 dl. barley flour
or ordinary white flour
suet
thyme

Boil lightly salted lamb's head or other salt meat with bone for 1-2 hours, according to amount. Remove the meat and clear the broth.

Peel and grate potatoes and drain, but retain the white sediment at the bottom of the drained off liquid. Mix into a dough with the flour and the oatmeal. It must not be too firm. Form the dump-lings with wet hands. If you want suet in them, stick a small piece inside each one. Gently boil the dumplings in the broth with a little thyme. Kohlrabi is traditionally served alongside, which have been cooked in the same broth for the last 20 minutes. Serve with bacon fat or melted butter, sausages, salted meats and kohlrabi – either puréed or diced.

The County
of Rogaland

Authority

The Nation

Melody: «Vi ære en nation vi med»

My life is first of all local
home must be some place.
The neighbourhood is communal
there my loved ones are.
But we live in a district
and if a promise has dimension,
we, as a clear conclusion,
a county must declare.

But a land is built up
with governing bodies.
Our Constitution has so far held true,
our flag is our rallying focus.
We have the red, white and blue
and stand fast on issues large and small.
And in the nation we have been granted,
our faith grows ever stronger.

Lars Chr. Sande

We have titled the photograph on the preceding page "Authority". It shows five people at the helm in Rogaland, representing the nation, the county and the municipality. The smooth functioning of a society is the reflection of the successful interaction between its authorities.

Front left we see Lieutenant Governor Kristin Lønningdal, senior public servant in Rogaland. Her duties include overseeing that the municipalities adhere to the Municipal Legislation. Behind her stands Major lt. Hjalmar I. Sunde, senior officer of the defense forces in Southern Norway, based at Jåttanutten. Next to him is Bishop Bjørn Bue, representative of the State Church in the See of Stavanger. Top right stands the Chairman of the County Council, Lars Vaage. The county Council has a great number of responsibilities in Rogaland, which we will come back to. And front right sits Mayor Kari Thu of Stavanger, the largest primary municipality in Rogaland, county capital and oil capital of the nation. They were all in charge in 1987, the year the book were first published.

10 years of growth

In 1986 the Rogaland County Council celebrated ten years of direct elections to the county government. Ten year old Astrid Norhus was chosen to symbolise the celebrity (photograph at bottom). The ten years were a time of great achievement, particularly whithin education and health. The new hospital was inaugurated during this time, in 1983. The County Council has built up a vast administrative system, not enough to meet all needs, but a great improvement nonetheless. In a few short years Rogaland emerged as a modern county, at a rate of progress outstanding in Norway.

The Council

The County Council carries on traditions dating back to the establiserment of Local Legislation in 1837. Howev, it was not until 1976 that the county government members were elected directly through local polls, at the same time as municipal elections took place. County taxation is also calculated directly rather than through the municipal budget, as was the case before.

The Rogaland County Council use almost 70% of its total budget – 3,3 billion kroner in 1987 – to cover health services. The main hospital, *Sentralsjukehuset i Rogaland* – Central Hospotal in Rogaland – alone has a budget of about 600 million kroner a year, more than what it cost to build hospital.

Haugesund also has a modern, well equipped hospital. Two smaller hospitals are at Sauda and Eigersund. The Rogaland psychiatric Hospital at Dale is being discontinued, to be replaced by psychiatric nursing home and new clinics in Sandnes and Stavanger.

The County Council has major responsabilities within communications and culture as well. It is indicative of its area of influence that the County Council's properties are insured for 2,5 billion kroner.

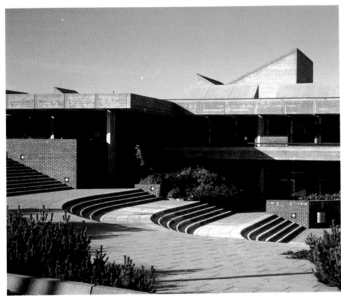

Smart new schools

The tertiary schools of Rogaland were getting old, tired and cramped. However, conditions are gradually improving as new schools join the force. Above, we see the Sola tertiary school. Left the Vardafjell school in Haugesund. The third scool is also in Haugesund: Haugaland tertiary school.

Central hospital

The next two pages show the Central Hospital in Rogaland, the county's largest employer with around 5000 employees. The aerial view was taken towards the main entrance. Between the two new buildings you can just see the old hospital built in 1928.

Photograph: Finn Stokke

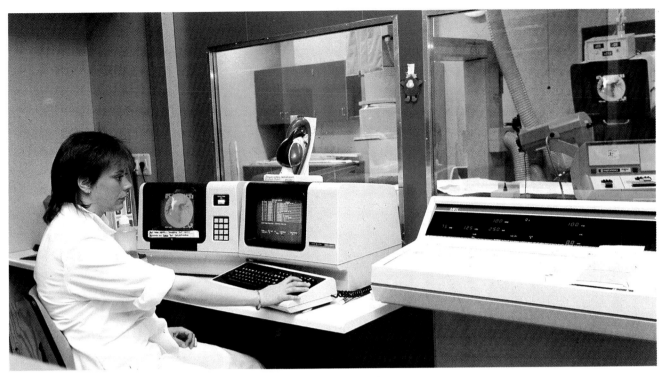

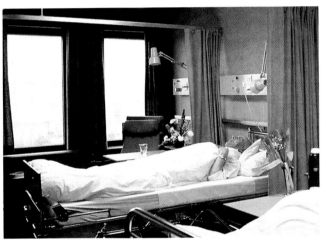

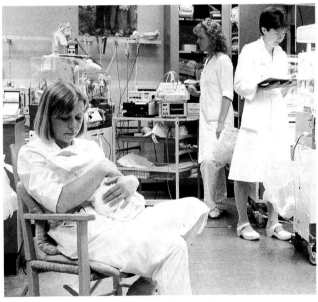

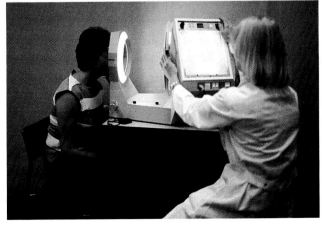

Stavanger

Stavanger's population in 1987 reached 93.500 inhabitants. The parishes of Hetland and Madla were incorporated in Stavanger municipality in 1965, in order to ease further expansion. Building space for homes and industry was running out within the old city limits and the annexation of the two parishes paved the way for the growth required by the oil industry in the next couple of decades.

Stavanger became a bishopric in 1150 and by the 1600's it was one of the most important towns along the Norwegian coast. The bishopric however, was transferred to Kristiansand in 1682 starting on a downward trend. The final blow came when the commercial charter was withdrawn in 1686.

Stavanger eventually recovered. When the first shipload of emigrants on board "Restauration" set sail for America on July 4th, 1825, there were about 4000 inhabitants. Herring had brought prosperity and growth to Stavanger in the previous decades. However, it was not to last; by the end of the 1870s the herring had vanished and in 1883 the economy crashed. A number of the large merchant houses of Stavanger went bankrupt. It was a time of despair, with no visible promise of relief.

Still, Stavanger people have never been able to afford the luxury of giving in to despair for long. They found that there was a living to be made canning food for the growing shipping industry, so canneries multiplied along the waterfront and in every available shed. Wherever herring was salted a while back, sardines were now canned. With Chr. Bjelland in the lead, Stavanger brisling sardines conquered the world

market, 50 million tins of sardines went out in just one year. Which, at say just 10 sardines per tin, makes 500 million sardines – laid head to toe by nimble Stavanger fingers. It provided occupation for the women of the town.

Shipping and ship building are also firmly part of Stavanger's history. In addition, Stavanger has always been a commercial centre.

The most abrupt transformation for the city came with the oil industry. Stavanger was chosen for the headquarters of Statoil and the Petroleum Directorate, plus a number of oil companies and related service companies.

When oil was first found, Stavanger had been in yet another period of stagnation. The days of the canning industry were numbered, and since then have become extinct. Today it is only at the Canning Museum where you can see how it was done.

The Norske Veritas building.

Above: Rosenkilde Place and harbour. Below: S/S Norway on a visit to Stavanger.

Previous page: Top: From old Stavanger. Below: The Norske Veritas building.

Utsira

With no more than 250 inhabitants, Utsira is Rogaland's – and Norway's – smallest municipality. It sits off the coast at a good hour's boat journey from Haugesund. Fishing and shipping have always been the economical mainstays of this group of islands and continues to be so now, in the oil era. Utsira's municipal coat of arms carries a lighthouse beacon as its symbol. This picture was taken during a celebration in 1985. Lars Vaage, County Council mayor, and the mayor of Utsira, Torbjørn Rasmussen, beat the drum on the occasion of the inauguration of the combination

post office, library and nursing home – where the two old timers in the centre photograph appear to be enjoying themselves.

The entire County Council came to Utsira to celebrate the opening of the new building. Moose steak and cloudberry cream was served on the occasion in the brand new reception hall. Can the little island community out in the ocean survive? They who live there are optimists; they feel their chances are all the better now for having such a valuable community centre. Photograph: Lars Chr. Sande.

Bjerkreim

Bjerkreim municipality is situated in Dalane – the valleys – centrally located between the highly populated areas of North Jæren and Egersund.

The national highway E-18 cuts through Bjerkreim and makes the distance brief to the urban centres of Egersund, Sandnes, Stavanger and Bryne.

The municipality has an area of 670 square kilometres and a population of 2300 people. The administrative centre is Vikeså which, along with the town of Bjerkreim, are the two urban areas in the municipality. Bjerkreim is an inland mountain town surrounded by varied landscape.

Agriculture is the most important source of income for the municipality. It is dynamic, particularly in milk and meat production. Fine grazing in the mountains have made this ideal for sheep as well.

The municipality has several newly established industrial concerns, among them a dairy, lumber yard, manufacturers of insulating glass and agricultural implements, electronics, ventilation systems, etc.

The municipality has large areas designated for holiday cottages and camping parks. We have a modern down-hill ski centre and, presently in the planning stages, a large, modern ski station with a stadium, ski shooting arena, ski jumping and several kilometres of prepared slopes.

Cultural life is varied and the population is active in a number of clubs and associations.

The narrow valley of Ørsdalen has finally been granted a road fit for automobiles. It had been totally dependent until then on boat traffic. The first of the boats came around the turn of the century, dragged up by muscle and brawn across land from Egersund. The last of the boats, Ørsdølen, has now become a veteran operated by enthusiasts, and can be seen on a fine summer Sunday taking tourists across the 200 metre deep lake.

Bokn

Bokn has been a strategic area throughout history. The name Bokn means a navigation point or landmark, this a junction between North and South Rogaland. Bokn has been densely settled from far back, right up to the boom-times of the herring. In more recent times the population had decreased but it is now on its way up again gradually.

In 1991, when the mainland connection to Tysvær via Kårstø and the ferry connection with the southern party of the county is established, Bokn will again be a strategically important junction between North and South Rogaland.

Bokn municipality is situated between Karmøy and Tysvær, and will be most conveniently located once the new coastal highway is open. The municipality consists of Western and Eastern Bokn, Ognøy and a number of smaller islands. The total area is 47,6 square kilometres of beachline which form fine natural harbours and points of beaty.

The population in the municipality is around 750 inhabitants, whith over half living around the urban areas of Føresvik and Alvestadkroken.

Bokn has always been a fishing community. In recent times traditional fishing has declined but fish farming is coming to take its place. Municipal authorities hope that this will play an increasingly important role in the community's economy.

The modern administrative centre of the municipality is at Føresvik, where there is a nursing home, bank and post office, as well as other services. The centre is next to a modern elementary school and a football field. The school building also houses a library and a nursery school. The municipality has a football team, music school, arts and crafts groups, etc.

The climate is mild and the vegetation consists mostly of heather. There is also some attractive forest area with deciduous and evergreen trees. Bokn also has several lakes which are good for fishing and the sea around Bokn is also rich in fish.

The standard of living in Bokn is good; it provides old and young with a sense of security. The elderly are taken care of through a nursing home and a well developed home help nursing system. Nursery school capacity is good and will be increased further. Many are involved in group interests such as handiwork, football, etc. Co-operative and mutual consideration among the population is one of the riches of this society.

The municipality has made building lots available at residential developments, but it is also possible to build on privately owned lots.

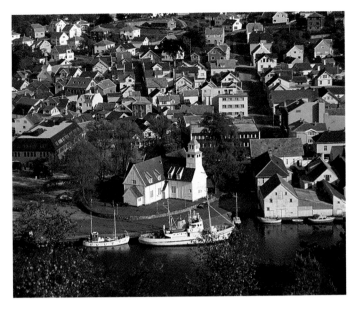

Eigersund

The municipality of Eigersund has 12,117 inhabitants and covers an area of 430 square kilometres.

Eigersund actually consists of three former municipalities: Egersund, Eigersund – which is the former Egersund agricultural parish – and Helland. The municipal administration is located at Egersund, which remains the name of the main, central town.

In 1746 Egersund was given official recognition as a regional loading harbour. The town's inhabitants had hoped for a trading charter, but this was pre-empted by Stavanger merchants. Commerce, fishing and shipping grew and lent importance to the little loading town. In 1847 an important step was taken: Johan Feyer founded the Egersund Fayancefabrik Co. which was to continue to prosper for 132 years. At its best time, the factory employed close to 550 people.

Large scale herring fishing ended around the 1950s, however, bigger vessels made it possible to fish in the North Sea all year round, giving the herring oil factories a new lease on life. Inspite of this, the fishing vessels and equipment have been taxed out of all profitability.

But Egersund has again sprung to life. Kværner Brug now has more employees than the Fayancefabrik ever had. Eigersund also has an important timber industry and a modern export slaughter house. A certain amount of mining is also done. The Bakkebø Sentralinstitusjon provides employment for a large number of people in caring for the mentally handicapped. Eigersund has two tertiary schools.

The Dalane Folkemuseum and the newly opended Fayancemuseum – pottery museum – have unusual collections and make Egersund an interesting town for tourists.

Above, to the right, we see the District Magistrate's estate at Slettebø, where the Dalane Folkemuseum has its main buildings. This lovely estate was the home of Magistrate Feyer, father of the founder of the Egersund pottery factory.

Below we see a glimpse of the main house at the Dalane folk museum, a spacious patrician home from the last century.

The Dalane Folkemuseum also has a collection of fishing implements at Sokndalstrand.

The landscape of Eigersund is varied, Nordre Sund is reminiscent of the mellow beauty of the south coast.

The Egersund Treplantingsselskap – Egersund tree planting company – has wooded the hills, providing fine hiking terrain.

Skadbergsanden beach is a popular place when summer now and then makes an appearance.

In the summer, Eigersund has a scheduled ferry route to Denmark. The town has a hospital combined with a nursing home. A psychiatric nursing home with an outpatient's clinic was opened in 1986.

The centre of Egersund town has undergone much renovation. A new pedestrian mall and the market area make it a good place to shop and meet people. Gjestehavnen – the guest harbour – allows waterborne shoppers to park their boats right in the centre of town.

Finnøy

Finnøy is an island municipality in Boknafjord, 20-30 kilometres north of Stavanger. With 15 inhabited islands the municipality is much divided, but bridges, ferries and express boats form a close bond between most of them. In the planning stages are serveral new bridges and an undersea tunnel to the mainland and between the islands.

Finnøy municipality has about 2780 inhabitants and an area of 106 square kilometres. The main Island, Finnøy – with its municipal centre of Judaberg – measures 25 square kilometres and has about half the total population.

Finnøy has long been an agricultural community and farming is still the most important livelihood. Livestock keeping and greenhouses mainly. Fish farming is in rapid development in the municipality, with several new installations on sea and land. The service industries are also growing, especially in Judaberg.

Finnøy municipality has an all-round cultural life, with many interest and study groups. In this context, two lovely stone churches from the 1100s need to be mentioned, plus a nearly 350 year old timber church.

Education in Finnøy is localised through necessity because of all the islands. A tertiary college is at Judaberg, offering courses in fish farming, health and social work, catering and serving. The municipality has a well developed health and welfare programme.

Fertile soil, mild climate, a number of sheltered harbours and good fishing areas, plus a rich social life have made Finnøy a desirable place to live. The municipality can offer fine, large building blocks on all the large islands. Finnøy's lovely nature and its fine shores make this municipality a popular excursion place.

Ved Sjernarøy kirke

Rødmalt er den gamle kirke,
kirken har gitt øya navn.
Pyntet ligger kirkegården
gravene gir mange savn.
Grønn er øya, Kyrkjøy kalt.
Kirken drysser livets salt.
Folk i sjal og vadmelstrøye.
gammel tid på Sjernarøyer.

Fuglesang i gamle eiker,
salmesang i kirkehus.
Bibelord som sinnet kveiker,
lovsangsord til orgelbrus.

Kirkehus med slekters gang
under lyd fra klokkers klang.
Hoder seg i andakt bøyer,
sinn seg mot det høye tøyer.

Rødmalt er den gamle kirke,
øya ligger vårlig grønn.
Solen drysser gull på sjøen
gjør naturen mer enn skjønn.
Fjellet topper seg på Tjul,
løvetannen lyser gul.
Folket seg med mangt fornøyer
på de fagreste blant øyer.

Lars Chr. Sande

350 year old Finnøy Church.

The ambulance boat at Forsand.

Forsand

Forsand municipality is a mainland community located at the southern entrance of the Ryfylke. The municipality is 840 square kilometres, extending from Lysefjord towards East and West Agder counties. Forsand has 950 inhabitants. Although it is on the mainland, short ferry trips are necessary to reach North Jæren in the west, and the rest of the Ryfylke in the north. However, this will soon be a thing of the past, since a new project to bridge Høgsfjord and Lysefjord, using the latest in underwater technology, is now under planning.

The municipality has a wealth of nature. The main attraction, the Pulpit Rock, has been a magnet for tourists for over 150 years. The new Lysebotn road has become another great tourist attraction, almost through coincidence; it was built as part of the power station project and not with tourists in mind. The road has 27 hairpin curves and a drop of 950 metres. The last section of road passes through a 1100 m. tunnel.

Hunting, fishing and outdoors activities are all available and snow is plentiful in the mountains. A rich cultural life is also available, being one of the municipality's prime concerns.

The dominant industries today are sand quarrying and power production, but the past few years have also seen a development of large fish farming centres, of which Aqua-Trading in Eiane is the largest. A factory at Helle – Kolbjørn Skulbry A/S – makes staircases with the aid of computerised technology. A number of smaller firms are also in business. A ground breaking project, Forsand Telestove A/S, took shape in 1987. It is to function as a centre of expertise in computer services for the municipal authorities, private firms, schools, private organizations and individuals.

Gjesdal

Gjesdal is an inland mountain community, situated between Jæren and Dalane about 30 kilometres south of Stavanger. It has an area of 617 square kilometres.

The municipality has been in rapid development the last few years. Population is on the increase and new enterprises are being established. Life is good in Gjesdal. We have practically limitless nature right outside our doors and the cultural activities organized by private interest and study groups seem endless. Service industries have also multiplied of late, so most necessities can be attended to within our own borders.

A total of 6600 people live in Gjesdal, 65% of them in Ålgård, the seat of the municipal administration.

Other urban settlements are Oltedal with about 700 inhabitants, and Gilja with about 200.

Gjesdal is an agricultural community with emphasis on livestock, particularly sheep. Most of the crops are used to feed our livestock.

Industry has become an important part of the local economy. The textile industry is the most important one, but we also have others such at timber, iron and metal, canneries, etc. Electric power is produced at these power stations at Maudal, Oltedal and Oltesvik.

Gjesdal is an attractve recreation area with wide open plateaus, mountains, valleys and lakes. A large number of cottages have been built and tourism is particularly active during the winter at the ski centres of Giljastølen and Østebødalen. Månafossen in Frafjord continues to thunder down the cliff as it has done in time immemorial. Kongeparken has become the biggest tourist attraction during the summer and we hope soon to provide the facilities for different types of water sports.

The municipality's road system is well developed with mostly hard-top roads. The road from Byrkjedal to Bjerkreim passes through the famous Gloppedalsura, said to be the scree with the largest boulders in northern Europe.

The photograph shows one of the old factory buildings of De Forende Uldvarefabrikker – built in a style that became popular in this country with the industrial revolution in the last century.

Textile industry at Gjesdal: De Forenede Uldvarefabrikker.

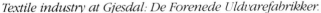

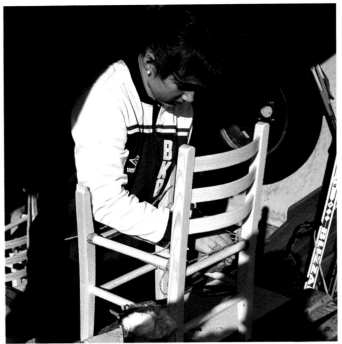

Making the traditional Jær chairs.

Hjelmeland

Hjelmeland municipality with about 2850 inhabitants is the second largest municipality in Rogaland. It has an area of 1092 square kilometres.

The centre of the municipality is the town of Hjelmelandsvågen. The name comes from the mountain called Hjelmen – the helmet.

Agriculture is dominant in the economy of the municipality. The farms produce milk, breed pigs, keep sheep and produce eggs. Fruit and berries have been cultivated for many years, while fish farming is a more recent venture.

Several new firms have become established in new industrial areas. the largest of these is the roof tile factory on Mælsøyrane in Årdal. Sand is quarried at several locations in the municipality, among them Årdal, Tøtlandsvik and Vadla.

The manufacture of traditional Jær chairs – upright pine chairs with rush seats – and of baskets woven of strips of wooden shavings goes back to the beginning of this century.

Hjelmeland's most remarkable building is Årdal's old church. It was built of logs in 1619 in the so called long-church style.

The Vigatun, on the road between Hjelmeland and Fister, is a well kept old farm complex. As it stands today it dates from 1821 but the oldest of the buildings, a smoke house, was built in the 1600s.

A large part of Hjelmeland is hilly or mountainous. Much of the watershed in this area is exploited by the power stations of Ulla Førre and of Lyse Kraft.

Haugesund

Haugesund is Rogaland's northernmost municipality. You can stand with one foot in Haugesund and the other in the county of Hordaland, a fact that is evident in the character of the town; the majority of the population stem from Sunnhordaland and Hardanger, rather than the Ryfylke. The economy is tied to Hordaland county as much as it is to Rogaland.

Haugesund is not only a regional centre for northern Rogaland but also the focal point for the approximately 150.000 people who live between the Hardangerfjord and the Boknafjord.

The economy has been based on the sea for generations; on herring, and shipping. However, within this past generation this has changed and it is now based on commerce, administration and education. Haugesund has proved to be an unusually successful merchant town; turnover per head is 50% above that of Stavanger, proving that the town serves a large area beyond it.

Haugesund has become a cultural centre, its highlight the Norwegian Film Festival, which is held in August each year. In addition, the hotel and restaurant industry has expanded to such a degree that the town has become one of the major congress centres in Norway. This provides employment in a new field.

The resources of the sea have changed. Fishing is no longer important, although here is still some herring business. However, a number of supply boats for the oil industry are operated from the town and Haugesund tankers are engaged on the Norwegian shelf. Although the town has not become home to any oil company or operations base, many enterprises – small and large – base their business on the oil industry. Quite a few of the town's inhabitants have found employment offshore.

The foundation for this solid economic development in Haugesund for the past 25 years has been a good communications network.

Not less than 6000 housing units, all of good quality have been built in the last twenty years, without any increase in population. About 4000 people commute to Haugesund each day.

Haugesund's future appears bright. In the past the town has had to rise or fall with the fate of an economy based on the sea, swinging between prosperity and times of serious need. The new Haugesund will be much more stable and can expect an even development. Our growth potential surpasses most other towns in western Norway.

Young people should take note of this and aim to be a part of Haugesund's future.

Amanda from Haugesund

The Amanda Prize of the Norwegian Film Festival in Haugesund is a statuette of a plump little woman with billowing skirts and an air of comfortable coquetry. She is not just a sculptor's whimsy, she is based on solid legend.

Amanda was a Haugesund mother of five children. She was their sole support, and they were hungry. Ingenuity was needed, but then this is not usually a quality found lacking in good Rogaland people. So, Amanda set to: she took a bit of yeast and a bit of sugar – familiar items to any housewife – and went into business supplying home brew to the sailors on board the ships in port.

That is the way Liv Ullman told it, anyway, at the 1987 Film Festival which she compèred.

Then, there is the version where song came before myth. To do with the Swedish sailors' song whose title happened to rhyme with Haugesund, borrowed in the entertainment hungry times after the war. The words were adapted, and Amanda became a lusty local belle of great generosity, celebrated in a song that delighted Haugesundians with all its familiar local allusions. It has much to say about red hot kisses and rosebeds, Eriksen's Pensjonat and the varied delights af a sailor's life, none of which translate – besides, would it even be proper? – so, suffice to say that

None were as good and round,
As Amanda from Haugesound.

The picture above shows old against new. The large blue building in the background is the Nordsjøhallen at Haugesunds Mekaniske Verksted.

The photograph at the bottom shows the annual May 17 regatta in Haugesund harbour.   *Photograph: Tor Brekke*

The old Vicarage has become the one of the most successful cultural centres in Rogaland.

Hå

Hå municipality is part of the Jæren district. It was established in 1964 by joining Nærbø, Varhaug and Ogna. Hå is an important agricultural community. A population of just under 13.000 people has settled mostly around the railway stations at Nærbø, Varhaug and Vigrestad.

The municipality has an area of approximately 255 square kilometes. Most of the almost 40 kilometre long stretch of coastline is straight, without islands or bays. In the northeast the Hå river runs through a flat landscape. Both this one and the Ogna river are good for salmon fishing.

Hå municipality has three well developed service centres: Nærbø, Varhaug and Vigrestad, of which Nærbø is the largest. The municipality's administration is at the Town Hall in Varhaug.

Hå has seven primary schools: at Høyland, Bø, Motland, Vigre, Varhaug, Vigrestad and Ogna.

Junior high schools are at Ogna, Vigrestad, Varhaug and Nærbø, and a tertiary school, Tryggheim, is located in Nærbø.

The municipality has well developed health centres at Nærbø, Varhaug and Vigrestad.

Jæren is one of Norway's richest archaeological fields. Of the total 5000 finds made on Jæren, about one fifth have been in Hå. The archaeological dig at Hå is located on a beach of round boulders, close to the old Hå Vicarage – *Hå gamle prestegård* – which has now been converted into a cultural centre. The Vicarage dates from 1787 and includes several annexes and out buildings. The complex has been extended with a restored "Jærhus" which is to house the books and manuscripts of the Rogaland writer Alfred Hauge, willed by him to the municipality of Hå upon his death.

The complex, built traditionally around a yard, is interesting in itself. In addition high quality exhibitions of art and regional themes are held here regularly, making the old Vicarage a popular place for family outings and one of Rogaland's most successful cultural ventures in recent times.

The municipality has a varied economy. Much of the industry is related to agriculture. Service industries cover most sectors.

Klepp

The municpality of Klepp is situated around the centre of Jæren, 20-30 kilometres south of Stavanger. Its surface area is 115 square kilometres, of which 15 square kilometres are water. Of the dry land area, about 80 square kilometres are agricultural land.

The heart of the municipality is Kleppe (Kleppekrossen), which consitutes a main communication centre. It is not long from here to the nearest station of the Southland railway and Sola Airport is only 15 kilometres away.

Most of the offices of public administration and services are under one roof at the modern town hall in Kleppe.

Agriculture has always been a prime interest; nature has been generous.

In addition to the traditional grazing and milk production, some of the land is devoted to crops of various kinds; there is breeding of fur bearing animals, pigs and chicken farms and a large greenhouse production of tomatoes, cucumbers, etc.

A number of general industrial enterprises have also followed in the steps of agriculture. The best known of these is Kverneland A/S (with Kyllingstad) and Serigstad A/S. The first dairies were established about one hundred years ago; Klepp municipality is one off the foremost in this branch. Norske meierier – the Norwegian dairies – have had a modern regulating warehouse and packing station for cheese and butter here, one of the largest in northern Europe. Norske Meierier also have an experimental dairy next to Høyland Meieri at Voll. The administration of Rogalandsmeieriet A/L is located at Klepp.

The building company G. Block Watne A/S, with Block Berge A/S, has its headquarters at Klepp. This firm is regarded as the largest of its kind in the country.

Høyang-Polaris at Orstad produce, among other things, kitchen utensils and saucepans. Many of the above enterprises also do a large export business.

Klepp has been culturally important through the ages. A number of archaeological discoveries form the stone age have been made here, more than anywhere else in the country. There are riches from later eras as well: Orre Church dates from the 1200s; at Tighaug a burial mound with the tomb of a woman from the migratory period was found, as well as the remains of 16 houses.

Even busy Klepp farmers have time out for a roadside chat.

Karmøy

Karmøy municipality has around 35 000 inhabitants and an area of 228 square kilometres. The name comes from the old "karm" – meaning shield; anyone who comes from the blast of the North Sea to the sheltered, "shielded" Karmsund sound knows that the name fits. The municipality extends from Feøy in the west to Førdesfjord in the east, and is 14th among the country's municipalities in population.

Fishing and agriculture has been surpassed by manufacturing and service industries. Norsk Hydro's aluminium plant on Karmøy is the largest in northern Europe, involved also in refining. Workshops, mechanical industry and the production of comestibles are other important contributors to the economy.

Karmøy is a communication centre for North Rogaland with regular air service, national ferry route for Boknafjord and express boat connection. The administrative centre of the municipality is in Kopervik, which is a lively business centre with the many advantages of a small town. Other important commercial centres are the former town-municipality of Skudeneshavn, and Åkrehamn and Norheim on the mainland. Other urban centres are Vedavåg and Avaldsnes.

Karmøy is rich in history, not least from the Viking age, when King Harald Hårfagre lived at the royal estate at Avaldsnes, where he eventually died. Olav's Church still stands there as a lovely reminder of those times. Just recently, a secret passage was discovered by archeologists there, which they ascribe to the residence of Harald.

The Visnes mine, which was northern Europe's largest mining community at the turn of the century, supplied a number of projects with copper, among them the Statue of Liberty in New York. The mine has

At Vedavågen fishermen's huts have been equipped for renting to tourists. Avid fishermen – and women – flock to Vedavågen in the summer, to try their luck and to experience the genuine Norwegian west coast fishing atmosphere.

From Karmøy to New York

The cover of the mining museum at Visnes, showing the closeness of the ties between Karmøy and the United States are.

been since transformed into an attractive museum and community centre. Another interesting museum is found at Skudeneshavn, in itself worth a visit for tourists. In addition, there are plans for opening a fisheries museum at Åkra.

Karmøy has well developed education facilities and a particularly active cultural life, proof of which are the large number of clubs and associations. Plenty of modern sports complexes permit the practice of most sports.

Kvitsøy

The municipality of Kvitsøy is located deepest in the Boknafjord. It consists of four populated islands and a number of small islets, as many as there are days in the year, it is said. 500 inhabitants make it the next to least populous municipality in the county. The islands have no woods, but are green and fertile and support a steady agriculture which includes breeding animals for fur.

Kvitsøy's traditions in fishing and shipping go a long way back. These occupations have now grown less important, but dependance on the sea prevails: fish and lobster farming and servicing the fishing fleet. There is also a fish depot, a fishmeal plant and a shellfish plant. In addition to some minor industrial activity, Kvitsøy Kringkaster – broadcasting – are the major employers. The municipality has land available for new enterprises.

With its "South Coast" type charm, the island is becoming increaslingly popular as a recreation area. A tourist/camp/school complex is now under construction. The municipality is well served by a nursing home, nursery school and sports facilities. There are a number of private organizations and the sports league is acquiring new, larger premises.

The muncipality expects a population increase of 0.5% by the year 2000. Land for new residential development will be made available adjoining already built up Leasundet and Ydstebøhavn. Work places will be increased and communication improved. At present, the municipality has a number of commuters who work on the mainland and whose ferry fares between Kvitsøy and Mekjarvik (Stavanger) are reimbursed by the municipality.

The are six daily ferry connections; travel time is 45 minutes.

Lund

The municipality of Lund has an area of 414 square kilometres. It is one of the inland municipalities of Rogaland, bordering West Agder. The municipality has 3.100 inhabitants, about half of whom live in the town of Moi. Moi is the administrative and commercial centre of the municipality, where the major industry is located.

Lund is served by an exceptionally good communications network since both the E-18 and the Southland railway cuts right through it. For travelling further, it is only half an hour's drive to Sola airport, or about 15 minutes to the ferry stop at Egersund.

Industry dominates in Lund's economy. Calculated in relative employment, Lund is the most industrial municipality in Rogaland. The largest concerns are the window manufacturer Johs. Rasmussen A/S with about 370 employees (in Lund), and the leather garment manufacturer Aleksander A/S with about 190 employees. In spite of this, agriculture is still important and a number of private and public service industries have also provided employment for a growing number of local people.

Lund municipality has well developed social services in most areas. Nursery schools are about sufficient to meet the demand and most schools have, or will soon have, new buildings. Health and welfare services provide all the usual services, in a local environment which has few serious social problems. Care of the elderly is particularly good. The short distance to Flekkefjord hospital is reassuring in case of illness or childbirth.

Most of the residential building in recent years has taken place in spacious, pleasant developments. It is still easy to find reasonably priced residential lots anywhere in Lund.

Lund's varied landscape, with extensive open spaces, lakes and rivers, provides a good bases for outdoor activities in summer and winter. Several mountain lakes have been seeded in recent years and now offer fine fishing. The municipality's inhabitants also enjoy a wide scope of recreational activities through sports and music clubs, religious groups and a number of other organizations.

Randaberg

It is 12 000 years since the first settlers came to Randaberg, which is believed to be one of the first places in the country to have had a permanent settlement after the ice melted. In those days the land was 25 metres lower than today, so parts of it were covered by the sea, leaving an archipelago.

The first of these settlers lived in *Svartehola or Vistehola* – the Black Cave or the Viste Cave – important tourist attractions today.

We would like to jump a few thousand years forward, to the middle ages to the times the nobleman Jon Torbergson. He was closely related to Norwegian royalty and played an important role in the society of the 1100s. At that time Randaberg was a parish with about the same borders as today. However, the plague robbed the population of so many lives that Randaberg could no longer afford to keep a priest, and it came under the jurisdiction of Stavanger parish.

Until 1922 Randaberg was a part of the Hetland administration becoming independent only after that.

Randaberg has been a typical farming community until recent times. In 1950 the population was about 2000, almost all of them employed in agriculture. However, in the last few decades industrial development has caught up and equaled agriculture – which continues as one of the cornerstones of the community's economy.

Randaberg is in the midst of a period of growth. As one of the North Jæren municipalities, we contribute towards making this region ever more dynamic. Oil is naturally a key word. Expansion of the service industries has been of great benefit for local inhabitants, providing access to many services locally.

Randaberg is about to realise a town-planning project without par in Norway: present development and construction is based on the results of a country-wide architectural competition.

Opportunities for recreation and outdoor life are plentiful in Randaberg: beaches, hiking and a nature park at Harestadmyra, presently under preparation.

Randaberg has a breadth of atmosphere, culture and economy which we are proud of, and which we gladly share with others.

Børaunen.

Rennesøy

Rennesøy municipality consists of six inhabited islands, two of them – Sokn and Bru – connected by a bridge. The total area is approximately 66 square kilometres. Population is 2504, with 1461 living on Rennesøy, 659 on Mosterøy, 206 on Bru/Sokn, 165 on Vestre Åmøy and 13 on Brimse.

Rennesøy has been settled for a long time. Its archaeology is one of the richest in the country.

Surviving from the middle ages are the buildings of the Ustein Abbey which was restored in 1969, and the old stone church at Sørbø, dating from around 1140.

Further, the Rennesøy Bygdemuseum – village museum – has collections from Rennesøy and Mosterøy, the "Bakken" croft, and old school house at Bru, and a recently restored windmill next to the Rennesøy junior high school.

It is a typical agricultural community; livestock and tomato cultivation are the most important. Many of the small greenhouses have now been replaced by large, automatised ones covering a total area of 85 square kilometres (over 20 acres). Milk production is above the national average. Pig and sheep farming also contribute to the economy.

52% of the population is employed within agriculture, 9% in industry, 7% in construction, 6% in commerce, 12% in shipping and other communications and 14% in service industries.

The Rennesøy nursing home and the Rennesøy nursery school are located just beyond Vikevåg centre.

Connection between Rennesøy and the mainland (Stavanger) is by car ferries and express boats (Westamaran). Recent residential developments (on Askje, Vestre Åmøy, Bru, Vikevåg and Østhusvik) have contributed to making Rennesøy a commuters's municipality, with a considerable number of people who live on Rennesøy and work in Stavanger.

Plans to join the islands to the mainland through a tunnel are likely to bring about great changes for the municipality.

maritime transport is growing. Sandnes also has a railway station equipped for container transport. The railway line goes to Kristiansand and Oslo.

The town of Sandnes is, first of all, a commercial centre. In recent years it has been much modernised, carefully conserving the old buildings. Development and modernising is still possible within the central town area.

Around 625 homes are built yearly, 60% of them single family homes. Most of the residential building is concentrated around the town centre.

Culture and recreation

Sandnes municipality is surrounded by fine recreation areas close to the centre. The Ims-Lutsi water system is suitable for swimming, hiking, canoening, camping, etc. Other areas are available for mountain climbing, jogging, orienteering, nature study, mushroom and berry picking.

The Rogaland Arboret, situated just south of the town, has become a popular excursion place.

Sandnes has an active sporting life; local cyclers, gymnasts, track and field clubs, volleyball and basket ball teams compete at top national levels.

Sandnes established a municipal music school already in the 1960s and takes pleasure in music. The people of north Jæren have produced operas locally for example in cooperation with the Norsk Opera. "The Merry Widow" and "Fiddler on the Roof" have been performed at the aula of the Rogaland Psychiatric Hospital at Dale for a large and enthusiastic public.

The photograph to the left shows Langgata.

Bottom: To live with music, it is best to start young. The music course of Lundehaugen school in Sandnes has helped launch some promising talents.

Sandnes

Sandnes is situated centrally in the Jæren region, at the innermost point of Gannsfjord. It has an area of 302.9 square kilometres of which 296,5 square kilometres is dry land and 6.4 square kilometres are islands and sea.

At the beginning of 1987 Sandnes municipality had 41.954 inhabitants. It is one of the fastest growing municipalities in the country. The workforce numbers 20.000 people. Of these, 60% work in service industries and 30% in industry and construction.

Industry

Outstanding is the Øglænd concern, manufacturing bicycles, textiles and developing robot systems.

Sandnes Uldvarefabrikk, Sandnes Kamgarn Spinnery make textiles, yarn and knitwear. Polaris make saucepans and other household utensils and Figgjo Fajanse is a well established china and pottery manufacturer.

Gann-Graveren make bricks and other clay products. The municipality has several building firms and oil related firms, as well as computer firms such as Scanvest and Norsk Data.

Norsk Biotech A/S is a pioneering enterprise where about 30 scientists do highly advanced research work on cells and gene technology.

Communication

Sandnes is located at the crossroads of Jæren. The inter-European highway E-18, the national highways N-44 and N-13 all run through the town of Sandnes, and a local roads system branches out from the town to the surrounding district.

Sandnes harbour has all necessary facilities for handling cargo;

Sauda

The Ryfylke town of Sauda lies at the head of the Saudafjord. In 1987 the population of the municipality was about 5500. Wooded and rocky hillsides form a southfacing bowl around Sauda.

It's a lovely spot to visit in any season. In the summertime with camping and fishing gear bound for the many mountain lakes – in wintertime on skis over one of the many mountain valleys in the area to experience the relaxation where Sauda residents and tourists shake off their everyday troubles.

Svandalen, with its ski lifts and alpine ski-runs has become more and more important for the local people. Winter tourism is a developing business. The downhill ski center in Svandalen can compete with others in the national and international market.

In 1914 Sauda was transformed from a tiny farming community into a thriving industrial community when A/s Saudafaldene won a concession to develop the Storelv water course for the production of electic power. Power deliveries to the foundry which was called EFP & Co. at that time, began on October 20, 1920. From that date onwards the foundry became a cornerstone of local employment.

Today the foundry still plays a vital role in local employment. The labor force of around 650 today faces tough international competition. In addition to this is the worldwide condemnation of the South African regime – the foundry's most important source of raw materials – which means that the labor force must strive to develop new products and rationalise work processes.

In recent years however Sauda has developed other mainstays. Besides the foundry A/s Statskraft, SI-glass A/s, Sauda Monteringslag A/s, Technor A/s and Fristad & Kalvik A/s, to name but a few, have built up an impressive array of technical expertise. A number of other enterprises have also been established to help keep Sauda a thriving community.

One of the most important bases for a vital society is education. The schooling opportunities are fine in Sauda which today is a learning center for the Inner Ryfylke region. There are five elementary schools, a secondary school and third level education in many disciplines.

Sokndal

The municipality of Sokndal borders Egersund to the west, Lund to the east, and Flekkefjord in Vest Agder county to the southeast. The coastline, including the fjords, is 48 kilometres long. The land climbs steeply from the shores, and fjords cut into the land creating good places for settlements and harbours. From east to west these are: Nesvåg, Nordfjord, Rekefjord, Løgevik, Sogndalstrand, Jøssingfjord and Åna-Sira. The municipality of Sokndal covers an area of approximately 295 square kilometres.

The population numbered 3487 at the beginning of 1987. Of this number, about 2000 live in Hauge i Dalane, which is the centre of the municipality and where the local administrative offices are located.

Bus connection to the surrounding district is good. Highway 44 between Egersund and Flekkefjord is the municipality's main artery. The municipality's internal road network is well developed.

Most employment is to be found in industry. There is mining, a crushing plant, asphalt work, foundry, fish industry and oyster farm. Commerce and service industries are well developed, as is the public sector. Many young people have found employment lately in the primary industries of agriculture and fisheries.

Sokndal municipality has an excellent hiking terrain and a lot of good sea and fresh water fishing.

Have you seen
– the Altmark memorial stone in Jøssingfjord?
– the old houses at Helleren in Jøssingfjord?
– Northern Europe's largest "rocking stone"?
– the Sokndal church?
– the fisheries museum and the old wooden houses at Sogndalstrand?
– the rock carvings at Haneberg?

If not, take a trip to Sokndal and you will see this, and more.

The famous downhill skiers Stein and Ivar Halsnes come from Sauda.

Sola

Sola municipality has an area of 69 square kilometres. It is located north on Jæren, east, south and west of Hafrsfjord.

Historically and traditionally, the economy of Sola municipality has been tied to the primary industries of agriculture and fishing. A gradual change has taken place, particularly in recent times, as a consequence of the development of the oil industry. Although agriculture is still important, it is the other industries which dominate now with their growth potential, development of new jobs, production and economy. As examples we can name the airport with its attendant activities, the oil refinery, service bases for the oil industry, docks, workshops, service companies, etc.

The municipality's administrative and commercial centre is located at Solakrossen. There are other urban areas within the municipality as well: Tananger, Sørnes/Grannes and Tjelta. Sola has a population of about 15.000 people.

Sola municipality has developed its services according to the tradition, al pattern, all of them with good facilities. In the last ten years large sums have been allocated for schools and cultural buildings. The most recent examples of this are the new Sola Videregående skole – the Sola tertiary school – which was opened in the autumn of 1985 and the cultural centre, opened in the autumn of 1987. The cultural life of the community is diverse, with over 100 active interest and study groups, most of them conducting their meetings in modern localities. Sports have received a lot of attention in recent years. In addition, Sola is proud of a most up to date libary. Three leisure centres for youth between 14-18 are also run by the municipality.

Tourists who visit Sola will appreciate the attractive beaches. Sola beach is particularly noteworthy as this is where bathers flock to, whenever Rogaland's summer weather permits. The beach is excellent for windsurfing, which is done year around.

Sola municipality is rich in archaeological sites as well. Public access to the most interesting of these is being improved at present.

The Shell refinery at Risavika was built before oil was found in the North Sea.

Strand

The municipality of Strand has an area of 215 square kilometres. It is situated on the mainland east of Stavanger in the idyllic Ryfylke region. The municipality has much to offer. Large and attractive building lots for the inhabitants, beautiful nature and plenty of social and cultural activities.

Strand is the principal centre in the Ryfylke region, owing to the size of its population and its communications facilities. It is also a main business centre.

The towns of Tau and Jørpeland have about 2300 and 4500 inhabitants, respectively. In all, 9200 people live in Strand. Jørpeland is considered the main town of Ryfylke, and this is where the municipality's administration is located.

Strand municipality has developed its services along the regular pattern, with good facilities in all sectors. Attractive building lots are a specialty.

Tertiary education of most kinds is available in the municipality. Rogaland county is erecting a new building for this purpose at Tau.

Commerce and the service industries have grown much in recent years. Jørpeland continues to be the business centre for neighboring smaller municipalities. The choice of merchandise and services is comprehensive, and viable under any comparison.

Cultural life is diverse and can accommodate all who want to develop their talents further. Adult education courses, sports and art activities are most popular, all conducted in modern localities.

Strand and the surrounding area offers grand nature and fine reacreational activities summer and winter. The choices are many, among them we can name the Ryfylke fjords for boating and fishing, and the hills for hunting and skiing.

All in the best Ryfylke quality.

Above the Jørpeland steel mill, one of the area's biggest employers.

Suldal

Suldal, with its 1752 square kilometres, is Rogaland's largest municipality. Its nature varies from attractive fjord landscape to high mountains where reindeer roam.

The main town is Sand, with good shopping facilities, a tertiary school with both general and trade courses, and a hotel by the fjord. The Ryfylke museum is also located at Sand.

Suldal municipality benefited greatly from the years it took to construct the largest power station in Norway. Population increased to over 4000, even 4200 in the summer of 1987, but a slight decrease is already noticeable since the completion of the project.

Suldal has been called the most industry-friendly municipality in Rogaland. This attitude created new jobs for the villages, among them at a barrel factory at Jelsa. Agriculture and forestry are also important.

The largest number of emigrants from Rogaland to the United States came from the Suldal region.

The cultural heritage of Suldal is of renown. One of the many

Tysvær

Tysvær municipality has an area of 419 square kilometres. It is situated centrally on North Jæren.

It is a municipality with much variety, with agriculture, timber production and modern industry, with hills and fjord and built up areas.

The most important livelihood until recently has been agriculture and timber, along with some fishing, but the scope of commerce and the service industries has increased in recent years. The gas terminal at Kårstø has created a number of new jobs in the oil industry. Moderately priced land for industrial development has contributed to a spread of small and medium sized businesses.

The municipality provides every facility to those who desire to settle here, with large residential lots in a number of attractive areas.

Aksdal is the municipality's administrative centre. it is situated at the traffic junction between highway E 76 and the start of the coastal highway.

Commerce and the service industries, as well as industry, have become established mostly along the E 76 in the Aksdal–Førdesfjord area, where the choice of merchandise and services is wide and competitive.

Tysvær has a population of 7.800 people, who enjoy the wide scope of cultural and recreational activities for all ages available in the municipality.

Attractive surroundings allow all outdoor activities, be they on sea or land. The number of fjords and the open sea are a delight for small boat owners. Fishing is plentiful, not just in the summer but in winter too, through the ice. And for simply communing with nature, there are still lakes and heather decked hills.

The names of famous people such as Cleng Peerson from Hesthamer and Lars Hertervig from Borgøy have spread the word of this municipality far beyond its borders.

The Tveit county agricultural college is located at Nedstrand.

attractions is the Kolbeitveitun. Johan Veka, a Suldal teacher, has been a cultural force in the inner Ryfylke for an entire generation.

The 120 million kroner new Suldal road brought many a remote farm out of isolation.

Suldal's salmon fishing is famous. The municipality is well represented in this book, with a photograph of the *Suldalsdampen* – the Suldal steamer – at the beginning and salmon fishing at Lågen as the last large photograph. Here we see the "bridal boat", an ancient Suldal tradition resuscitated as a cultural event. We can thank pastor Inge Bruland for the good pictorial documentation of Suldal; he is an expert at being in the right place at the right time, with a camera.

Time

Time municipality is located in central Jæren, extending over 182 square kilometres. Without a coastline, it is an entirely inland community. The landscape varies from the typical flat Jæren vistas to hilly terrain towards the municipality's eastern borders.

Time has population of 11.400 inhabitants, 75% of whom reside in urban areas. Agriculture, which used to be the mainstay, now employs no more than 16% of the work force. The rest work in industry, construction, commerce and service industries.

The municipality's administrative centre is at Bryne, which has a population of about 6000. Bryne has a number of industries, a good variety of commerce and service industries – which are in steady expansion. Further, Bryne is a centre for tertiary education; two schools catering to about a thousand students each, offer a variety of lines.

Other urban areas are Kverneland with about 1.800 inhabitants, Lysefjell with 1.400 and Undheim centre with about 500 inhabitants.

The municipality has a good location; at a short distance from the facilities of Stavanger and Sandnes, close to Sola airport, and to a large variety of recreational activities, among them swimming along the Jæren beaches, hiking in woods and fields, and skiing in the surrounding hills.

In addition, the municipality has a rich cultural life with emphasis on music and athletics, as well as plenty of clubs and associations. Football has contributed to making Bryne a household name throughout the country.

Vindafjord

"Old" Imsland, Vikedal, Vats, Sandeid and half of Skjold – in all 443 square kilometres of Mother Earth – were joined on 1 January, 1965 into one municipality called Vindafjord. The name, as the land, is beautiful. Politically, the region belongs to North Rogaland, although it might be more fitting to talk of "Vindafjord in the Ryfylke". Feel free to think of it whichever way seems right.

Either way, the municipality lies half way between Haugesund and Sauda, settled by some 4.900 good Vindafjord people. And, although the municipality does not quite grow by an inhabitant a day, it still does increase now and again. Thus, the size of the population grows, slowly but steadily.

What about the urban centres of Vindafjord? The municipality's goal is for the even development of five small centres: Ølmedal, Vikedal, Sandeid, Vats and Skjold. At present most of the public administration is located at Vikedal, with a few offices in Sandeid. However it has been decided to make Sandeid the future administrative centre of the municipality. Work to accomplish this is under way at present.

The economy of Vindafjord is based mainly on agriculture, but the municipality has a number of crafts and industries as well. A base for building and equipping oil platforms has been established at Vats. Thus, the oil age has reached Vindafjord.

About 20 kilometres of the E 76 highway goes through Vindafjord. The municipality has a good communications system in all directions, and excellent express boat route to Stavanger.

She collects folk music
Rogaland used to have a poor reputation in the way of folk music. However, the results of a search made by Ruth Anne Moen in the Ryfylke suggests that this is far from true. After graduating from the Rogaland Music Conservatory, Ruth Anne Moen was given the task of collecting folk music in the Ryfylke for the local Ryfylke Folk Museum. Based on her results, we should make haste to search further before the traces disappear altogether.

Ruth Anne Moen is a fine Hardanger fiddle player. She is seen here playing music to suit the landscape.

Photograph: Terje R. Lea

Highlights

By Susan Tyrrell

Life in Rogaland flows fairly evenly from day to day, season to season. That is one of its strengths, that the traditions are firm and the way clearly marked. Now and then though, that evenness is broken into by a special event, a high point that moves life onto another plane; that stands out way above the rest as an exclamation mark.

Rogaland has had her share of highlights in recent years; events that become yardsticks to measure new ones against. The new road to Lysebotn, for example, is undoubtedly a highlight, not only of scenic thrills but of road building science. Then, the famous people we have had the opportunity to welcome, the trophies, the festivals, the coming of age in education, culture, industry – they are all highlights.

We will take a look at some of them. The selection is arbitrary and far from complete. But highlights they are.

Sissel Alice Hanstad clad in the "bunad" the traditional dress of Rogaland with little Espen photographed on 17th May 1987.
Photograph: Rune Tollefsen

The road to Lysebotn

Talk about highlights!

Actually, blue and green lights, icy deep lights, gold spangled fjord lights. Then again, soft focus mist lights and dense rolling storms edged in silver brilliance.

Rogaland nature is the abode of light. You can visit the same spot time after time, yet think you have just made a new discovery. Because the light plays tricks. It moulds and transforms shapes, changes distances, creates – or hides – features seemingly on a whim.

We, who are fortunate enough to have Rogaland around us, know that it is almost impossible to take a bad photograph of our scenery; with boring regularity, snapshots turn out poster perfect every time. Yet, there was perhaps the occasional suspicion that our scenery may not be quite as dramatic as some of the famous beauty spots around Norway; possibly ours is a scaled down, tamer version. But there is more to beauty than drama, we would say.

Until the Lysebotn road was opened. With over two dozen hairpin bends cascading down the mountainside, Rogaland gained a scenic wonder.

The awe-inspiring grandeur of that road, with its treasure of the ever changing fjord held out as a reward at the end, is the proud equal of any landscape, anywhere in this country.

Lysebotn: light in the deep. It was aptly named.

The road was built by the firm of Bertelsen & Garpestad of Egersund and Kruse Smith of Stavanger.
Photograph: Fjellanger/Widerø.

Stavanger celebrated its grandest cultural event between May 6th and 11th, 1983. A monument to commemorate the union of Norway's many small fiefdoms into one kingdom, Fritz Røed's "Three Swords", was unveiled in the presence of H.M. King Olav V. A gala opening concert was held at the new Concert Hall at Bjergsted park.

This tradition laden town held a "Kielland Banquet", where the local writer Alexander Kielland (long deceased) descended from his pedestal for an evening, and entertained guests together with the *Stavanger Jomfrustiftelse's* choir. Texts and music were by the orginator of the Festival, Lars Chr. Sande.

Photograph: Egil Eriksson, Øyvind Ellingsen and Odd Kielland.

STAVANGER
FEST
DAGER 6.–12. mai 1985

Red carpet occasions

Scholars, royalty, artists – they come to Rogaland now and then. They tend to be received with genuine pleasure rather than with pomp and circumstance; Rogaland enjoys playing host.

Take the time **Queen Beatrix of Holland** spent a packed five hours in Stavanger on a day in May of 1986. She was met by King Olav at Sola airport, she attended the opening ceremony of a Norwegian/Dutch oil seminar – which was officially opened by her husband Prins Claus – and she was whisked off to the sight-seeing boat Clipper in Stavanger harbour where she was regaled with flowers and band music and the acclaim of Stavanger's 400 Dutch residents.

☆

Nobel Prize-winner Elie Wiesel's visit left us all the richer. The uncompromising chronicler of the Holocaust spoke to a celebrity-studded audience at a gala arranged in his honour.

"We are either persecutors or victims, there is no in-between," he said. "We must learn from the horrors of the past in order to avoid new horrors."

The path we must take now is "tolerance combined with moral responsibility," said one of the greatest living humanitarians on an evening in May in 1987, at Bjergsted Concert Hall.

☆

In September of 1986 **Sweden's King Carl Gustaf,** visited North Jæren along with a six member delegation from the Swedish Academy of Engineering Sciences, to view the area's oil activity. It was a private visit, they were Statoil's guests.

☆

At lower right is **Crown Prince Harald** with the cornerstone for the Petroleum Directorate. It was on the 10th of May, 1984 and the buildings were inaugurated in January of 1986.

Photograph: Jonas Friestad.

The Emigration Festival

800.000 Norwegians emigrated to other lands between the years 1825 and 1930. About one third of Norway's population at the time.

The very first of these was a small group of Quakers who sailed from Stavanger harbour on July 4th, 1825. 52 people stood on the deck of the little sloop "Restauration", said farewell to their past and turned to face an unknown future in an unknown land.

The descendants of the 800.000 Norwegians who left home to seek their fortunes have now grown to some 4 million; equal to Norway's stay-at-home population. These second and third generation Norwegians showed every indication of wanting to keep up the ties, or to renew them.

This is cause for celebration. Stavanger organized an Emigration Festival for the first time in 1986, to give a proper welcome to these overseas Norwegians returning to find their roots. Stavanger became the Heritage Gateway to Norway.

Along with a summer-long concert season, exhibitions, lectures and outings organized by both hosts and guests, was the establishment of a serious institution: the Emigration Center. A research library and genealogy center containing all available records of the Norwegian emigration, plus books on local history from around the country, church records, emigration protocols, correspondence and press clippings.

Rendering homage to the first shipload of emigrants leaving for the new country. A theater tableau by Stavanger harbour on the opening day of the first Emigration Festival in 1986.

Photograph: Pål Christensen

All of Halsnøy

They had no band at Halsnøy, Finnøy, to strike up for a May 17th parade. Even so, the village turned out, 150 strong among young and old – the littlest ones riding on a trailer across the springtime-green island that looks towards the blue mountains of the Ryfylke.

Halsnøy is a little society on the advance. Young people move home and take over their family farms. The population has grown and the May 17th parade will be longer year by year.

Photograph: Pål Christensen.

Nearing
St. Hans

It is mostly sunny pictures that one finds in a book full of coloured photographs. To leaf through one of these is to leaf through only highlights. But reality can be long between one sunny day and the next, particularly in Rogaland. The weather gods have their games and allow spring to slide through one minute, only to cover it with snow the next. It takes time, but eventually spring does come – and the dandelions turn meadows to gold. The dandelion is the messenger: midsummer is coming and the sun will sit at its highest. And once the sun turns, it is hailed in the ancient manner in Rogaland as elsewhere in the country – but here the celebration is likely to take place under conditions more like autumn than summer.

Now and than the weather gets it just right and then mid-summer's eve, the Eve of St. Hans, is a mellow and translucent joy.

When the sun rides low it is time to light the bonfires, as a symbol of the sun's route around the world and a reminder that we should not let these days of sunshine slip through our fingers.

Photograph: Thomas Gjesteland.

Nato meeting in Stavanger

Stavanger was suddenly the centre of the world. Television sets in dozens of languages spoke, at length and with familiarity, about what was going on in Stavanger. Scenes of Breiavatnet lake were beamed into living rooms across the seas, to top level foreign government offices and fly-specked Mediterranean bars.

May 14-15, 1987 Stavanger hosted a meeting of NATO defence ministers, held in order to discuss an agreement on nuclear disarmament for Europe.

Fourteen defence ministers of NATO countries, including General Secretary Lord Carrington and the defense minister of the United States, Caspar Weinberger, came together for two days of talks at the Atlantic Hotel. Their presence caused the transformation of the peaceful and easy-going town of Stavanger into a high security

Flags, police and curiosity.

USA's Minister of Defence Caspar Weinberger.

zone with police reinforcements from the entire country, plus anti-terror troops standing by.

The brief meeting is calculated to have cost Stavanger about 6 million kroner, which includes the rental of 50 brand new white Volvos for attending VIPs.

Photograph: Jonas Friestad.

The Nato Ministers of Defence.

Rex Rodney – champion of trotters

One of the best in the world, Rex Rodney is a champion among trotting horses. He wins trophies with such regularity that it is not an event that is the highlight, but the protagonist himself.

Thorleif Thu, his owner, placed him in the care and training of Kjell Håkonsen at Sviland, and within two years Rex Rodney was winning practically every race on home ground, at the Forus tracks. True, he flubbed it in the Gold Division's finals at Bjerke, but perhaps just to prove he is not a myth

after all. There are other tours – to Sweden and the United States. Håkonsen believes in patient development. In the two years Rex has been in his care he has ingrained in him a winner's attitude, a pleasure in doing well.

"Rex is not in top form," trainer Håkonsen tends to say, "but he is certainly better than he has ever been".

For a horse that has come first in 30 of a season's 34 races, that is not bad.

Photographs: Pål Christensen and Jan Soppeland.

The school swings over the Petroleum Directorate and lands at the Teachers Training College.
                                        Photo: Guro Waksvik

A school-house flies across a century

Education in Rogaland has come a long way in one hundred years. You can see it at a glance at the Ullandhaug education complex.

Among sprawling modern buildings that house the district college, library, the hotel school and the teachers' training college: among buildings where some of the most advanced methods in oil technology are taught and where research into the methods of the future are conducted, sits a little white frame house, the size of a country school.

That is just what it is; a monument to the Rogaland Department of Education, to show the progress made in a hundred years.

It is a typical rural school house from the 1870s, which sat at Sør Fogn in the Ryfylke and gathered under its roof – in one room – local children of all ages for the few years that they could be spared from working on the farm.

Then, one day in September of 1986, the little school house was picked up by a helicopter – weighing 8 tonnes even with the roof and the loose objects removed – and was flown to Stavanger. There it was carefully deposited on new foundations on the lawn in front of the Stavanger Teachers' College at Ullandhaug. To highlight the distance we have come.

Sisters in song

When the municipality of Klepp celebrated its 150th year of local self-government plus the town's 450th anniversary in the spring of 1978, there were festivities to fill a whole fortnight. Part of the programme was an amateur competition led by Sissel Kyrkjebø. A girl from Klepp, Berit Mæland, won first place. Here she gets a good hug from her sister in song from Bergen. The people who heard her singing, backed by choir and orchestra at the Stavanger Concert House, thought she had a true talent. It seems obvious that talent blooms on the West Coast.

Photograph: Jon Ingemundsen

Veteran cars across Tronåsen

The road across Tronåsen, along the border between Roga-land and West Agder, used to be the great proving ground for drivers until after the war, when a road was built down by the Lunde lake. Now the old road across Tronåsen is open for traffic in the tourist season. In the photograph, veteran cars are puffing up along the steep and curving sections, amidst lovely landscape. Lund municipality has a tourist attraction to be proud of.

Photograph: Jonas Friestad.

A man called Emelankton

Emelankton Aadnesen of Nærbø stands behind the counter of this shop in Nærbø in the summer of 1987, as he has stood there since 1915. There are thousands of items on his shelves, and the 98 year old shopkeeper – who wears no glasses – finds the one asked for instantly. Through the years he has sold bicycles, fishing gear and gramophone records. As a matter of fact, he could still have a 30's record around here somewhere.

They don't make bicycles like they used to, says Emelankton. He still rides one though, firm and straight as a

youth. It is his son Andreas standing in the background towards the top of the picture. Emelankton's brother Randulf is responsible for the park at Nærbø, page 176.

Photograph: Jonas Friestad.

World champion/
European champion

When Erling Trondsen from Sola was four years old a veranda collapsed on him. The little boy's two legs had to be amputated. Today Erling Trondsen swims with astonishing speed and agility, setting world records in handicapped swimming. He has been awarded both Sola's and the County Council's culture prize.

Photograph: Fredrik Revfem.

Klepp girl Bjørg Storhaug waves the Norwegian flag at Krosshaug at Klepp. She is a member of the Norwegian women's team that became World champions in football. Bjørg is a farmer, she is eldest daughter and heir. She is also handy with cars and tractors that need fixing.

Photograph: Pål Christensen.

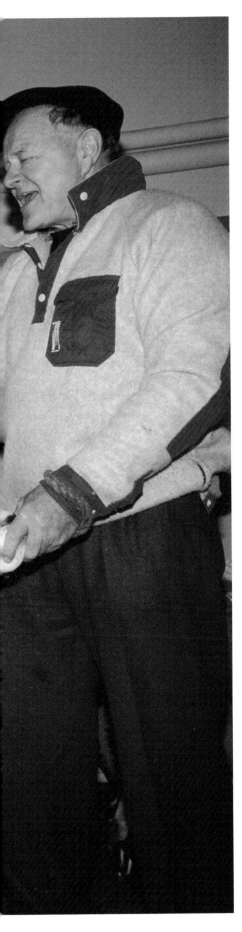

Bryne æ best!

That's how the home town fans cheer their team. It is no exaggeration, either. Bryne's football team came away with the Champion's Cup from Ullevål, scoring 0-1 in extra time. It was the grandest day these Jær folk had since the railway was officially opened in 1879. Some 7000 people were out to welcome the bold Bryne players home. The picture above shows the happy goal scorer, Kolbjørn Ekker, together with Else Finseth.
   Photograph: Knut S. Vindfallet.

Bryne supporters came all the way from the agricultural college at Ås, with a mascot sheep, here being ridden by goalie Lars Gaute Bø. Beside him stands football giant Arne Larsen Økland.
   Photograph: Pål Christensen.

From the whole word...

By Joan Felicia Henriksen

Rogaland has, historically, been quite resigned to its sons and daughters leaving for distant lands where there were greater opportunities. This southwestern section of Norway has been poor through most of its history. Then oil was discovered in the North Sea and Rogaland was where the jobs were to be found. Norway became the new land of opportunity.

In 1964 the oil men began arriving, most of them wearing cowboy hats and speaking with a Texas or Oklahoma drawl. Soon their wives and children followed. An American school was started and the new subdivision where they all lived was named "oil hill". In 1971 there were 900 foreigners living in Rogaland and working in the oil industry. On June 23, 1972 Stavanger Aftenblad, the local daily newspaper, recognized the growing English speaking community's needs by beginning a twice weekly page of local and national news in English. By 1974 efforts were beginning to be made to register all the foreigners in Rogaland and the first count, that year, showed the total to be 4000.

Americans most visible

The most visible new group may have been the Americans, but citizens of many other nations were also finding their way here. People from countries such as Turkey, India and Pakistan had begun coming to Norway looking for work in the late 1960's.

Inevitably there were vast differences between those who came looking for work from countries in trouble and those sent here on a temporary basis by companies hoping to get rich on Norwegian oil. The oil workers are people who have lived in exotic countries all around the world. They know they are here for an average of three years, so aren't very motivated to learn the language. They bring their world with them in company paid shipments and move into company housing. They tend to be highly educated, very well-paid, secure and outgoing.

French and British schools

Ekofisk was discovered in 1969 by Phillips Petroleum Co., an American firm, so it followed that at first the oil community was dominated by Americans. By 1973, however, there were 30 oil companies established in the area. A French school began in 1972 with 27 students – by 1987 there were 270. A British school opened in 1977 with just a few students in rented quarters. By 1982 there were enough to justify building and opening their own school which has since been expanded. As the 1986/1987 year began there were 240 students at the British school.

Immigration stop

In 1975 an immigration stop was put into effect. Even so there were 6,983 foreigners living in Rogaland in 1976. By the end of 1986 the total was 13,751 from more than 50 countries. Twelve percent of all foreigners in Norway in 1986 lived in the one county of Rogaland. Of this figure 6,634 were from English speaking countries. Today the Norwegian who grew up learning "Oxford" English has learned to

Father Christmas visits the little ones at the British shool in Stavanger.
Photo: Knut Upstad

Reza and Marion from Iran came to Haugesund as refugees. They came via Turkey and had a lot of help in the beginning.
Photo: Erik Østberg

understand the Australian, Canadian or South African variety as easily as that from Houston or London. Despite predictions to the contrary, which are made every time the price of oil goes down, the foreign community in Rogaland grows yearly.

Although the immigration stop slowed down the numbers of persons from some countries trying to come here for work without specific tasks that demanded their talents, the number of refugees and asylum seekers began slowly to increase.

Rogaland international

Rogaland has become international. On any sunny day you can hear five or six languages in the marketplace. Ten years ago you could go out to eat Norwegian or Chinese food. Today it's possible to choose between restaurants specializing in Mexican, American, French, Italian and Japanese delicacies, in addition to Norwegian and Chinese. Ten years ago it was almost impossible to buy foreign grocery products. Today a Rogaland family is just as likely to be dining at home on tacos or pizza as salt lamb or cod.

Norwegians join in enthusiastically to celebrate the In-

dian New Year in October, Guy Fawkes Day in November, the Turkish National Day in April and the American 4th of July. All the foreign schools march enthusiastically in the Children's Parade on May 17th, celebrating Norwegian Constitution Day.

A runaway success

The Saturday Cafe at the International Culture Center (which used to be called the Immigrant Center) has proven to be a runaway success. Each Saturday a different ethnic group serves a "native" meal and the tables are jammed with people of all nationalities eager to experience something new. There are more Norwegians in the American Square Dance Club some years than there are Americans, and an equal number of foreigners devote free time to learning Norwegian folk dances.

Foreign companies sponsor Norwegian cultural events and a Norwegian-French cultural center has become a garthering spot. Batiks from Sri Lanka are exhibited one day in a Norwegian gallery and the British Amateur Theater Group presents a melodrama the next at the American school. *(Cont'd. pg. 248)*

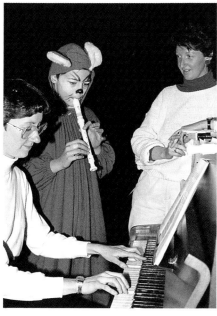

American Shool

One of Norway's best equipped school buildings, the Stavanger American School's first complex under one roof was inaugurated in 1982. Here we see Arne Rettedal, former Stavanger mayor and popular Rogaland politician, delivering a commencement address.

Photograph: Ellingsen.

Members from 35 nations

The Stavanger Petroleum Wives Club with its 700 members from 35 nations has become a local fixture. The women stage a yearly Carnival drawing huge crowds and an equally popular yearly Arts and Crafts Show. In addition to providing a support group for their members they have donated thousands of kroner to local philanthropies.

Life is good in Rogaland today, for everyone, so perhaps it isn't surprising that many foreigners are choosing to stay. Most of those making Norway their home find jobs with Norwegian companies, perhaps marry a Norwegian.

Vikings from Norway went out and conquered other lands. Then the ships went out with trade goods and later with emigrants fleeing poverty. Today the tide is going the other way. Norway in general and Rogaland, in particular, are attracting settlers from all around the world.

Friends: Deepika Rai from India and Hanne Håvardsten .
   Photo: Jon Ingemundsen.

From Asia and Africa

Stavanger has given refuge to many Vietnamese boat people. Their good adjustment has been aided by the Catholic Church. The picture above is from a Vietnamese nursery school.

Omar Njie came from Gambia in Africa, to become a farm worker at Røyneberg in Sola.

Photograph: Jan Ingemundsen.

Carnival fun

As carnival flows throught the Stavanger streets, there is no way to tell who is a foreinger and who isn't.

The carnival craze in Rogaland started out big: 15.000 paraders the first year. Rain drowned the 1986 parade and by 1987 it was a small group of merrymakers that took the streets.

Carnival brought customs from distant lands to a coast with a reputation for rather reserved people. These reserved people let their hair down colourfully enough to do justice to far warmer climes.

Photograph: Jon Ingemundsen and Pål Christensen.

Waffle vision

My waffel iron
makes waffles
with five hearts.
A delicious
golden brown
joined in a circle and
glowing warmly
like a little sun.
Waffle hearts
should symbolise
humanity on
the globe's
five continents
on the day
they have reached
the goal of
solidarity.
Together we
will have developed
just ways
to share our resources.
The aroma of fresh
waffles tickles
the nostrils.
Freshly baked, golden
with blackberry jam.
Heart by heart.
Can there be a better
Sunday tea-time treat
in Paradise?

Lars Chr. Sande

In the picture right are people from five continents whom the oil industry brought to the shores of Rogaland. From left: Bridgit Wilson, Australia, Mary Owusu and Afua, Afrika, Siew Bee Leung, Asia, Michelle, Mirabel and Nathalia Powell, Europe, and Debbie Griggs, America.
Photo: Jan B. Henriksen.